Best Easy Day Hikes
Atlanta

Help Us Keep This Guide Up to Date

Every effort has been made by the authors and editors to make this guide as accurate and useful as possible. However, many things can change after a guide is published—trails are rerouted, regulations change, facilities come under new management, etc.

We would appreciate hearing from you concerning your experiences with this guide and how you feel it could be improved and kept up to date. While we may not be able to respond to all comments and suggestions, we'll take them to heart and we'll also make certain to share them with the authors. Please send your comments and suggestions to the following address:

The Globe Pequot Press
Reader Response/Editorial Department
P.O. Box 480
Guilford, CT 06437

Or you may e-mail us at:

editorial@GlobePequot.com

Thanks for your input, and happy trails!

Best Easy Day Hikes Series

Best Easy Day Hikes
Atlanta

Ren and Helen Davis

FALCON GUIDES

GUILFORD, CONNECTICUT
HELENA, MONTANA

AN IMPRINT OF THE GLOBE PEQUOT PRESS

We dedicate this guide to the many staff and volunteers who preserve and maintain the parks and greenspaces we enjoy.

FALCONGUIDES®

Maps created by Ryan Mitchell © Morris Book Publishing, LLC
TOPO! Explorer software and SuperQuad source maps courtesy of National Geographic Maps. For information about TOPO! Explorer, TOPO!, and Nat Geo Maps products, go to www.topo.com or www.natgeomaps.com.

Library of Congress Cataloging-in-Publication Data
Davis, Helen, 1951-
  Best easy day hikes, Atlanta / Helen Davis, Render Davis.
     p. cm. – (Falconguides)
  ISBN 978-0-7627-5290-4
  1. Hiking–Georgia–Atlanta Region–Guidebooks. 2. Atlanta Region (Ga.)–Guidebooks. I. Davis, Ren, 1951- II. Title.
  GV199.42.G462D38 2010
  917.58'231–dc22

                                                2009024078
Printed in the United States of America

10 9 8 7 6 5 4 3 2 1

Contents

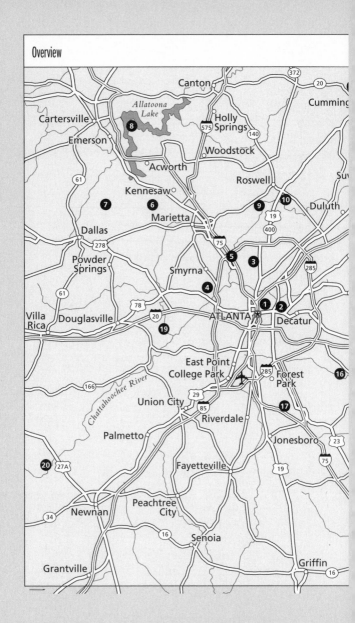

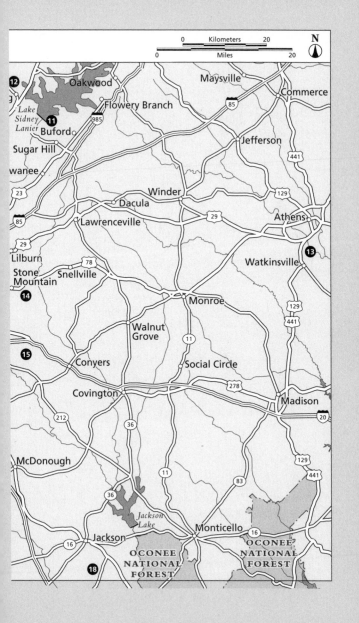

Introduction

Atlanta has long been touted as the City of Trees, and despite dramatic population growth both within the city and its surrounding suburbs, Atlanta still offers many easily accessible woodlands, parks, and greenspaces suitable for family outings or more rigorous treks. Wherever you are in Atlanta, there are destinations to suit your interests, from mountaintop vistas and paths along rushing streams to urban parkways great for a jog or bicycle ride, or historic sites linking us to those who came before.

Atlanta and the surrounding area is in the heart of the Southern Piedmont (*pied mont* means "foot of the mountain"), one of four distinct geological regions of Georgia. The others are the Ridge and Valley of northwestern Georgia, the Blue Ridge in northeastern Georgia, and the Coastal Plain stretching southward to the Atlantic Ocean from the fall line that marks the boundary between the piedmont and the plain.

The piedmont is crisscrossed by a network of streams and rivers, most with their headwaters in the mountains, flowing toward the Atlantic Ocean or the Gulf of Mexico. For more than 10,000 years, these waterways and surrounding valleys served as migration and trade routes for ancient peoples moving southeastward and, more recently, for Euro-American settlers traveling north from the coast to the interior. The result is a landscape that is both geologically complex and rich in human history.

The hikes profiled in this book trace diverse piedmont landscapes on peaks such as Kennesaw, Red Top, and Sawnee Mountains; along granite outcrops at Stone, Arabia, and Panola Mountains; across river and stream valleys found along the Chattahoochee and Oconee Rivers; and through rolling, wooded hills at Laurel Ridge, Reynolds Nature Preserve, and Dauset Trails. Two excellent sources for readers interested in learning more about the area's rich geological history are the award-winning *New Georgia Encyclopedia* (www.georgiaencyclopedia.org) and the University of Georgia Department of Geology Web site at www.gly.uga.edu (select "About Us" and click on "Georgia Geology").

For us, a walk in the woods has always been a way to escape the hectic pace of urban living, to recalibrate our lives to be more in synch with nature's rhythms, and to share our love of the outdoors with family and friends. Because of its climate, vibrant city life, and its easy access to mountains, woodlands, and waterways, Atlanta has long been considered one of America's most livable cities. We hope that this guide may be a small contribution to sustaining that reputation into the future.

Weather

Located more than 1,000 feet above sea level and in the heart of the Southern Piedmont, the Atlanta area is representative of a subtropical climate characterized by hot, humid summers and relatively mild winters. Historically, Atlanta has experienced approximately 50 inches of annual rainfall; however, recent droughts have yielded less rainfall, contributing to lowered lake levels, stressed forests, and tightening restrictions on water usage.

Given the mild climate, Atlanta is blessed with good weather for hiking during every season of the year. Autumn is notable for the vivid colors of changing leaves, while winter often opens vistas through leafless trees. Spring in Atlanta is internationally renowned for the glorious palette of dogwoods and azalea blossoms, and summer offers rich greens of hardwoods and pines in full foliage, punctuated by brightly colored wildflowers.

Safety and Preparations

Nearly all of the trails profiled in this guide are within an hour's drive, or a little more, from the city. When choosing a hiking destination, consider the trail location, hike distance and difficulty, weather, times of traffic congestion, and personal or family interests. In every case a little advance planning will make your hike both safe and enjoyable.

Clothing

Moderate weather in the Atlanta area offers enjoyable hiking at any time of year, provided you dress accordingly. Hot and humid summer days call for breathable fabrics, a hat, and sunscreen, while layers of warm clothing and outerwear can take the chill out of a winter hike. Weather can change quickly, especially in summer, so it is wise to stuff a windbreaker or rain jacket in your pack. When hiking with children, they often need to be reminded to add a layer as their bodies are affected by the weather more quickly than adults.

Shoes and Socks

While hiking boots are great for the hikes profiled in this guide, you may find that lightweight all-terrain walking shoes will be just as suitable. Also, don't forget to include a pair of good-quality hiking socks, usually made from wool or a synthetic blend, that offer better cushioning, moisture wicking, and less chance of blistering than cotton socks do. It is also a good idea to break in your boots or shoes on shorter hikes before hitting the trail for a longer trek.

Packs

For a short hike on a spring day, a fanny pack with side pockets for water may suffice. If you are planning a longer walk or will be carrying extra clothing, a camera, binoculars, field guides, snacks, and water, a daypack should serve you well. For comfort, choose a pack with well-padded shoulder straps and a hip belt, an easy-access main storage area, and external pockets for the gear you want at your fingertips. You may also want a pack with an external lashing system to store a jacket within easy reach. If you will be carrying several pounds of gear, choose a pack with a chest strap to keep the weight close to your body, placing less strain on your lower back.

Day Hiker's Checklist

A few essentials for a safe and fun hike:

- ❏ A comfortable pack
- ❏ Water
- ❏ High-energy snacks
- ❏ A trash bag
- ❏ GPS unit or compass, map, trail guide
- ❏ Sunscreen, sunglasses, and a hat
- ❏ Insect repellant (spring and summer)

❏ First-aid kit (carry an antihistamine if you are allergic to insect bites or bee stings)

❏ Rain gear

❏ Extra layered clothing for cold weather, including hat and gloves/mittens

❏ Camera, binoculars, field guide

❏ Watch

❏ Cell phone

Personal Safety

While the overwhelming majority of other trail users are also seeking outdoor recreation and enjoyment, it is always wise to be alert to your personal safety on the trail. A few tips to consider:

- Carry a cell phone.
- Notify friends or family of your plans.
- Be alert to your surroundings and others sharing the trail.
- Carry a whistle and/or pepper spray.
- Call 911 if you observe people acting suspiciously.
- Hike with companions to share the experience. If you wish to join a group, check out listings of hiking clubs in the back of this book.

Trail Regulations/Restrictions

Most of the trails in this guide are located on public lands (federal, state, county, or city parks), and each has regulations that must be followed for both your safety and for protection of the environment. While some parks are free, others charge a fee for daily use, with longer-term passes available. In addition, note hours of operation and allow yourself ample time to enjoy the hike before a park closes for the day. Review the Hike Specs for each trail for details.

Zero Impact

Given Atlanta's growing population and the limited availability of greenspaces, local trails can sometimes be crowded. To preserve and protect the landscape for your family and others, we ask readers to abide by the following "zero impact" principles:

- Leave with everything you brought.
- Leave no sign of your visit.
- Leave the landscape as you found it.

We would even go a step further and urge you to pack out any trash you find along the way, being mindful that it is not only unsightly but may also endanger the wildlife you may have come to see.

Also, stay on established trails, avoiding the temptation to take shortcuts or trample on fragile vegetation. And don't pick flowers or collect rocks or other souvenirs that will diminish the experience of those who follow. The familiar phrase "take nothing but pictures and leave nothing but footprints" sums up what it means to tread lightly on the land.

Land Management Agencies and Organizations

In addition to the local and county parks, the major land management agencies in Georgia and the Atlanta area are:

National Park Service: Southeast Regional Office, 100 Alabama St. SW, 1924 Building, Atlanta 30303; (404) 562-3100; www.nps.gov

U.S. Army Corps of Engineers: Lake Sidney Lanier, http://lanier.sam.usace.army.mil/

Georgia State Parks and Historic Sites: 2 Martin Luther King Jr. Dr. SE, Suite 1352 East Tower, Atlanta 30334; (404) 656-2770; www.gastateparks.org

PATH Foundation: P.O. Box 14327, Atlanta 30324; (404) 875-7284; www.pathfoundation.org

Public Transportation

Although Atlanta does not yet have an extensive network of public transportation, a number of the trails in this guide may be reached by mass transit from one or more of the following systems:

Metropolitan Atlanta Rapid Transit Authority (MARTA): The system offers bus and light rail service for the city of Atlanta and portions of Fulton and DeKalb Counties. Information and route maps are available at www.itsmarta.com; (404) 848-5000.

Cobb Community Transit (CCT): This bus service network connects locations within Cobb County and links to the MARTA system at two rapid rail stations. Information and route maps are available at www.cobbdot.org; (770) 427-4444.

Gwinnett County Transit (GCT): This system offers express bus service to major destinations within the county and to several MARTA stations. Information and route maps are available at www.gwinnettcounty.com; (770) 822-5010.

Georgia Regional Transportation Authority (GRTA) Xpress: Authority buses link twelve metro-area counties with Atlanta. Buses only operate Monday through Friday. Information and route maps are available at www.xpressga .com. The Web site also offers links to other county transit agencies.

Trail Finder

Best Hikes with Children

Best Hikes for Scenic Views

Best Hikes for Water Lovers

Best Hikes for Nature Lovers

Best Hikes for People-Watchers

Best Hikes for History Buffs

Best Hikes for Wildlife-Watchers

Best Hikes with Dogs

Map Legend

═══⑧═══	Interstate Highway
──⑲──	U.S. Highway
──㉞──	State Highway
────	Local Road
▬▬▬▬▬	Featured Trail
- - - - -	Trail
┝━┿━┿━┥	Railroad
∼∼∼	River/Creek
⌇	Marsh/Swamp
▭▭	Local/State Park
▭▭	National Forest/Battlefield
✈	Airport
🛶	Boat Launch
⌣	Bridge
▲	Camping
•—•	Gate
❷	Information Center
▬	Inn/Lodging
🅿	Parking
▲	Peak
⛩	Picnic Area
■	Point of Interest/Structure
🍴	Restaurant
🚻	Restroom
☎	Telephone
○	Town
⓫	Trailhead
🏞	Viewpoint/Overlook
💧	Water
⋛	Waterfall
♿	Wheelchair Accessible

1 Piedmont Park

For more than a century, this 186-acre park north of downtown has served as Atlanta's "common ground," hosting Confederate veterans, presidents, musicians (from John Philip Sousa to the Allman Brothers), baseball games, and the first football game ever played in Georgia. The landscape, designed by the Olmsted Brothers, was commissioned for the 1895 Cotton States and International Exposition. Piedmont's dog park is among the nation's top ten. At the northern end are the Atlanta Botanical Garden (ABG) and the fifteen-acre Storza Woods, one of the largest vestiges of mature hardwood forest in the city. (Storza Woods is accessible free of charge.)

Distance: 4.6-mile loop with a lollipop to Storza Woods
Approximate hiking time: 3 hours
Difficulty: Easy to moderate
Elevation gain/loss: 92 feet
Trail surface: Grass, pavement, mulch, and asphalt
Best season: All year
Other trail users: Inline skaters, bicyclists
Canine compatibility: Leashed dogs permitted; dogs may run free in the gated dog park
Fees and permits: None
Schedule: Open daily 6 a.m.–11 p.m.; guided tours 11 a.m. Sat
Maps: USGS *Northeast Atlanta* and *Northwest Atlanta.* Maps also available from the visitor center or at the Piedmont Park Conservancy Web site.
Trail contacts: Piedmont Park Conservancy, P.O. Box 7795, Atlanta, GA 30357-0795; www .piedmontpark.org. City of Atlanta Department of Parks, Recreation, and Cultural Affairs, 675 Ponce de Leon Ave., 8th Floor, Atlanta 30308; (404) 817-6788; www .atlantaga.gov. Atlanta Botanical Garden, 1345 Piedmont Ave., Atlanta 30309; (404) 876-5859; www.atlantabotanical garden.org.

Finding the trailhead: Located 3.0 miles north of downtown Atlanta, Piedmont Park is 0.8 mile east of I-75/85 at the 14th and 10th Streets exit (exit 250). To reach the Piedmont Park/Atlanta Botanical Garden parking deck, follow 10th Street east for 1.4 miles to Monroe Drive. Turn left (north) and drive 0.8 mile to Worcester Road. Turn left (west) on Worcester Road and travel 0.2 mile, through a short tunnel, to the parking deck (fee charged). Exit the parking deck by Magnolia Hall (Piedmont Park's 1940s-era special events facility), and descend to the starting point by the Park Street bridge. There is also street parking along 10th, 11th, and 12th Streets and commercial lots nearby. The park is also easily accessible via short walks from either the 10th Street or the Arts Center MARTA stations. **GPS:** N33 47.168' / W84 22.284'

The Hike

You may begin your hike through Piedmont Park from many points. We have chosen to start by the Park Street Bridge, accessible by a 0.1-mile walk from the parking deck. From the bridge, bear left and descend to the meadow. During the Cotton States Exposition, which drew more than a million people, this was home to Buffalo Bill Cody's "Wild West Show." It later served as a nine-hole golf course. At the base you may walk under the bridge to the adjacent, gated Dog Park (this will add about 0.2 mile to the hike) or bear right on the path around the meadow.

At 0.5 mile the path reaches an access point from 10th Street by Park Tavern (former golf course clubhouse). Continue to the right, closing the loop and ascending to the park's road (closed to automobiles). Cross and walk out on the Lake Clara Meer Bridge to see the gazebo. Turn around and descend the steps on the right to a gravel path bordering the lake. Turn left along the shore to a platform offering views of the water and midtown Atlanta skyline.

Climb steps to the left and cross the road, joining the paved Oak Hill trail as it ascends past a sculpture dedicated to former South African president Nelson Mandela, toward 10th Street. Above the Charles Allen Drive entrance, the path bends right along a ridge with panoramic views of the park. Bear right at 1.5 miles and descend on a long switchback to the park visitor center near the 12th Street entrance. If the building is open, view the exhibits and enjoy the view from the deck.

Ascend steps north of the building and walk through the Isamu Noguchi–designed playground, meandering beneath hardwood trees to the park's entrance gate at Piedmont Avenue and 14th Street. Pause to admire the Peace Monument, erected in 1911 to commemorate reconciliation between the North and South in the half century after the Civil War. Descend steps and cross the Active Oval's recreation fields, past a gazebo. Continue down a second set of steps to an activities area with a pool, bathhouse, and playground. Turn left, following the roadway past the tennis center, toward the Atlanta Botanical Garden.

Across from the garden's entrance, turn right and enter gated fifteen-acre Storza Woods. A lightly traveled, unblazed loop trail follows a 0.5-mile course through the woodland. At the completion of the loop, retrace your steps down the roadway to the parking deck.

Miles and Directions

0.0 Begin the hike at the Park Street Bridge. (GPS: N33 47.168' / W84 22.284')

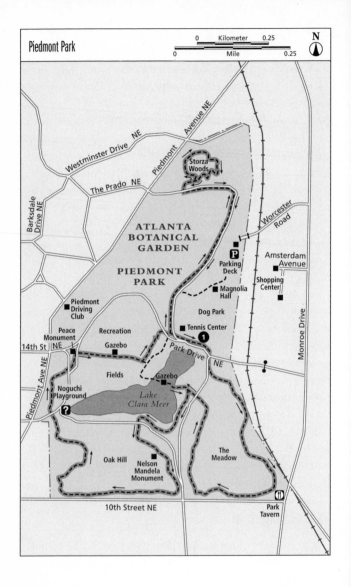

0.5 Arrive at the Meadow Trail intersection near 10th Street and Park Tavern.

1.0 Arrive at Lake Clara Meer Bridge and Gazebo.

1.4 Arrive at the intersection of Meadow Trail at Charles Allen Drive entrance.

1.7 Arrive at the Meadow Trail intersection with 10th Street access. (GPS: N33 46.920' / W84 22.678')

2.1 Arrive at the visitor center at the 12th Street entrance.

2.4 Stop at the park entrance at 14th Street to view the Peace Monument. (GPS: N33 47.185' / W84 22.636')

2.7 Arrive at the bathhouse, pool, and playground area.

3.2 Enter Storza Woods. (GPS: N33 47.482' / W84 22.394')

4.6 Arrive back at the starting point.

2 Fernbank Forest

Nestled in the valley of Peavine Creek and along wooded upland slopes, sixty-five-acre Fernbank Forest is a true rarity, a vestige of old-growth, virgin forest only a few miles from the heart of a major city. Families come to meander along paved trails beneath 200-year-old hardwoods, pause at overlooks and beside ponds, and reconnect with the natural world. Also on the grounds, the Fernbank Science Center offers exhibit halls, classrooms, a library, a world-class planetarium, an astronomical observatory (open Thursday and Friday evenings), and an aerospace education laboratory.

Distance: 1.5-mile interconnected loop trail
Approximate hiking time: 1 hour
Difficulty: Easy with some hills
Elevation gain/loss: 133 feet
Trail surface: Asphalt and rock
Best season: All year
Canine compatibility: Dogs prohibited
Fees and permits: None
Schedule: Forest hours 9 a.m.–5 p.m. Mon–Fri (summer); 2–5 p.m. (winter); 10 a.m.–5 p.m. Sat year-round; closed Sun and holidays. Contact the center for science center and observatory hours.
Maps: *USGS Northeast Atlanta.* Maps also available at the science center.
Trail contacts: Fernbank Science Center, 156 Heaton Park Dr. NE, Atlanta 30307-1398; (678) 874-7102; http://fsc.fernbank.edu

Finding the trailhead: From I-75/85, exit onto North Avenue (exit 249) and travel east for 2.3 miles. Turn left (north) on Moreland Avenue and drive 0.2 mile to Ponce de Leon Avenue. Turn right (east) and follow Ponce de Leon Avenue for 2.1 miles. Just before traveling beneath an arched railroad bridge, turn left (north) on Artwood Drive and drive 0.2 mile to a right turn on Heaton Park Drive. Fernbank Science Center parking is on the left. **GPS:** N33 46.696' /W84 19.137'

The Hike

Exit the back door of the science center and descend to the gatehouse by the fenced entrance to Fernbank Forest. Sign in and walk a few yards ahead, where you will turn right onto the Easy Effort Trail, which follows a level course along the edge of the woods. Turn left and follow the fenced edge of the property, passing a trail intersection on the left at 0.25 mile. The path begins a steady descent, past an old home (Hodgson House) that serves as staff offices. From that point, the path continues down, at times steeply, on a long switchback that was once the home's entrance drive, to Peavine Creek at 0.6 mile. An intersecting trail exits to the left, but continue straight across a bridge. Turn sharply left and ascend heavily wooded slopes.

The path bends right and, at 0.7 mile, passes a trail leading away to the left. Continue straight a short distance, then left to climb over a ridge (the trail straight ahead leads to the site of the nineteenth-century home of Colonel Zadock Harrison, whose daughter, Emily, saved the forest from development). Reach the Funderburke Overlook at 0.9 mile to enjoy a panoramic view of the forest from the wooden platform. Retrace your steps to the intersecting trail you passed earlier. Turn right and descend, at times over exposed rocks, to a pond named to honor Fernbank's first forester, Walter Huntemann, at 1.1 miles. Pause at the pond-side pavilion to view exhibits about local wildlife and the Peavine Creek watershed.

Ascend to the main path and turn right to begin a steady climb. At 1.3 miles turn left on a short side trail to a sheltered pavilion in the heart of the forest. Return to the main trail and turn left, continuing upward. You will soon pass

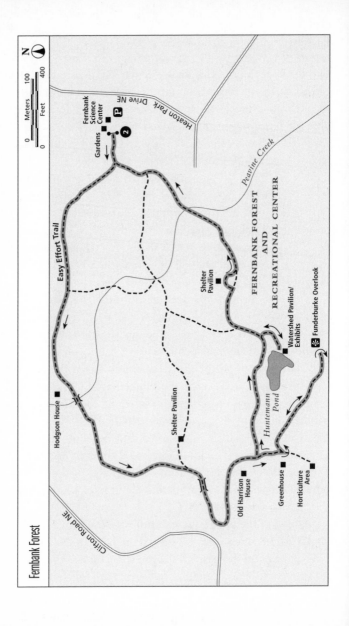

Fernbank Forest

an intersecting path at 1.4 miles, before reaching the fence and gatehouse at 1.5 miles. Before returning to the science center, explore the native plant gardens, water garden, and composting demonstration site.

Miles and Directions

0.0 Begin your hike by the gatehouse. (GPS: N33 46.696' / W84 19.137')

0.6 Cross the bridge over Peavine Creek. (GPS: N33 46.635' / W84 19.460')

0.9 Enjoy the woodlands view from Funderburke Overlook. (GPS: N33 46.560' / W84 19.339').

1.1 Relax and view the exhibits at Huntemann Pond.

1.3 Soak in the sights, sounds, and smells of the forest at the sheltered pavilion.

1.5 Return to the gatehouse.

3 Chastain Park PATH Trail

One of north Atlanta's favorite play spaces, 260–acre Chastain Park features a golf course, sports and recreation fields, a tennis center, a swimming pool, an equestrian center, picnic pavilions, and a playground. Nearby are the renowned Chastain Park Amphitheater and the Galloway School campus (private), whose original building was once the Fulton County alms (poor) house. The paved path meandering around and through the park is part of the network of PATH trails found in various areas around Atlanta.

Distance: 2.9-mile loop
Approximate hiking time: 1.5 hours
Difficulty: Easy with some hills
Elevation gain/loss: 165 feet
Trail surface: Concrete path with some sections of packed dirt
Best season: All year
Other trail users: Runners
Canine compatibility: Leashed dogs permitted
Fees and permits: None

Schedule: Open during daylight hours
Maps: USGS *Northwest Atlanta* and *Sandy Springs*. Maps are also available online from Chastain Park Conservancy.
Trail contacts: City of Atlanta Office of Parks, 675 Ponce de Leon Ave., Atlanta 30308; (404) 817-6744; www.atlantaga.gov. Chastain Park Conservancy, www .chastainparkconservancy.org.

Finding the trailhead: From in-town Atlanta, drive north on Peachtree Road to Buckhead. At the intersection with West Paces Ferry Road, take the left fork on Roswell Road. Travel north for 1.6 miles to Powers Ferry Road and turn left. Drive another 1.6 miles to West Wieuca Road and turn right. Street-side parking is available along West Wieuca and by the swimming pool.

From I-285, travel south on Roswell Road (exit 25) for 2.7 miles. Turn right on West Wieuca Road and drive 0.4 mile to Lake Forrest

Drive. Cross Lake Forrest and park on the street. **GPS:** N33 52.823'
/ W84 23.249'

The Hike

While you may join this loop trail at any point, our hike
description begins by the PATH sign embedded in a boulder at the corner of West Wieuca Road and Lake Forrest
Drive. Almost immediately after starting southward on the
paved trail, begin a descent along the edge of a sports field.
At 0.1 mile skirt the outfield fence of the Northside Youth
Organization's Little League "Field of Dreams," featuring
seats from now-demolished Atlanta-Fulton County Sta-
dium, former home of the Atlanta Braves.

Just ahead, the trail descends steeply on a switchback,
past a rest area, and across a footbridge. The path ascends a
gentle rise offering a panoramic view of the North Fulton
Golf Course. At 0.4 mile the path is bordered on the right
by a high fence that protects pedestrians from errant golf
shots. Continue past a spur trail leading to the Katherine
Murphy Memorial area overlooking Nancy Creek. After
crossing another bridge the path follows the edge of the golf
course on a gentle climb. At 0.9 mile the trail bends to the
right away from the road and descends to a narrow valley.

After crossing a third bridge, ascend, fairly steeply, through
a wooded area with picnic tables and a rest stop with a marker
honoring former Atlanta mayor Ivan Allen. Continue to climb
past the 1940s-era American Legion Post at 1.1 miles. The
path bends to the right along the southern edge of the golf
course and descends past a pavilion to Powers Ferry Road.

Along the shoulder of Powers Ferry, follow a dirt trail
as it climbs over a ridge and descends to another crossing of
Nancy Creek at 1.6 miles. History buffs may want to pause

to read the historical markers describing a cavalry battle near this site during the Civil War. Continue gently climbing to West Wieuca Road at 2.0 miles and pause at the rest area by the North Fulton Tennis Center.

Cross West Wieuca and turn right, below Chastain stables, then left along Pool Road. Climb through the parking area by the pool to rejoin the PATH Trail, exiting to the right at 2.3 miles. Follow a meandering path between a small pond and Galloway School. After a gentle descent, the trail climbs a switchback to Troy Chastain Parkway. Turn right and follow the road as it climbs, reaching the high point of the walk at 2.6 miles. Continue past picnic pavilions until the PATH Trail exits right and descends past the playground. A short distance ahead, the trail bends right, following Dudley Lane back to the starting point on West Wieuca Road at 2.9 miles.

Miles and Directions

0.0 Enter the PATH Trail by walking south, past a large boulder, on the paved path at the intersection of West Wieuca Road and Lake Forrest Drive. (GPS: N33 52.823' / W84 23.249')

0.1 Pass NYO Little League's "Field of Dreams."

0.4 Reach the level path along the edge of the golf course.

0.7 Pass the Katherine Murphy Memorial rest area.

1.1 The trail passes the American Legion Post before turning west along the golf course. (GPS: N33 50.768' / W84 23.331')

1.6 Note the historical markers at the bridge crossing at Nancy Creek.

2.0 Reach a rest area by the North Fulton Tennis Center.

2.3 Turn right from the parking area on the PATH Trail along the edge of a pond.

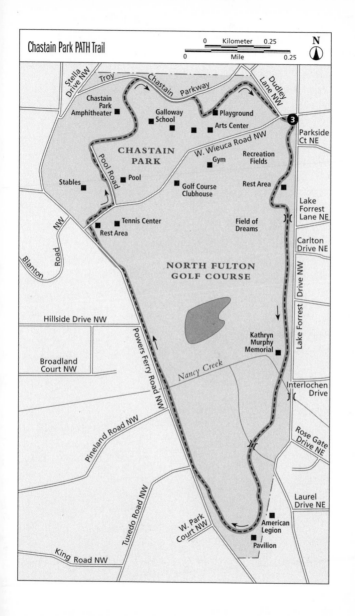

2.6 Arrive at the highest point along the hike, with a view of the park and city skyline. (GPS: N33 52.660' / W84 23.505')

2.7 Descend past the playground.

2.9 Arrive back at the starting point.

4 Silver Comet Trail: Mavell Road to Floyd Road

One of the region's finest "rail trails," the Silver Comet follows the former route of a passenger train that ran from New York City to Birmingham, Alabama. Developed by the PATH Foundation in partnership with state and county agencies, the multi-use trail, which stretches along the old railway bed, reaches the Alabama state line, where it connects with the Chief Ladiga Trail, providing a 101-mile-long pedestrian path that links suburban Atlanta with Anniston, Alabama. An attraction along this section of the trail is Heritage Park, with foot trails leading to ruins of the nineteenth-century Concord Woolen Mill, old Concord Covered Bridge, and a nature center pavilion.

Distance: 4.2 miles point to point

Approximate hiking time: 2 hours

Difficulty: Easy due to distance and gentle grade

Elevation gain/loss: 152 feet

Trail surface: Asphalt, concrete, with compacted soil and wooden boardwalk on side trails

Best season: All year

Other trail users: Runners, bicyclists, and inline skaters

Canine compatibility: Leashed dogs permitted

Fees and permits: None

Schedule: Trails open daily during daylight hours

Maps: *USGS Mableton*. Maps also available from the PATH Foundation Web site.

Trail contacts: PATH Foundation, P.O. Box 14327, Atlanta 30324; (404) 875-7284; www.path foundation.org

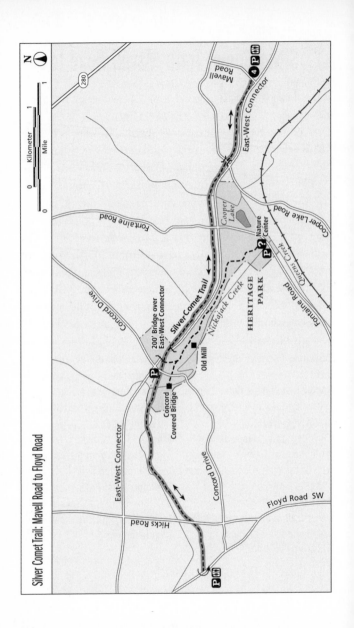

Silver Comet Trail: Mavell Road to Floyd Road

Finding the trailhead: From Atlanta, travel north on I-75 to I-285. Go west on I-285 for 6.7 miles to South Cobb Drive (exit 15). Turn right (north) and drive 1.8 miles to Cooper Lake Road. Turn left (west) and travel 0.7 mile to Mavell Road. Turn left (south) and drive to the road's end at the Silver Comet parking area.

To reach the Floyd Road parking area from I-285, follow South Cobb Drive north for 0.4 mile to the East-West Connector (GA 3). Turn left (west) and drive 5.8 miles to Floyd Road. Turn left (south) and travel 0.7 mile. The Silver Lake Depot parking area is on the right. **GPS:** N33 50.503' / W84 31.037'

The Hike

From the Mavell Road parking area, the trail gently descends to the west through a wooded area and crosses a bridge at 0.7 mile. It follows a mostly level course to a trestle bridge crossing over the East-West Connector at 2.3 miles. A short distance past the bridge, a foot trail on the left descends through Heritage Park to the Concord Mill Ruins. At the ruins the path to the right leads to the 140-year-old Concord Covered Bridge, while the path to the left winds along Nickajack Creek to a wetland boardwalk and beyond to a nature center pavilion and satellite parking area. A round-trip to see these attractions is an additional 3.0 miles.

Continue on the Silver Comet Trail, past an access trail to Concord Road, and through the railroad tunnel beneath Hurt Road at 3.0 miles. The path proceeds west, crossing Hicks Road and reaching Floyd Road at 4.2 miles. The Silver Comet Depot store and parking area will be on the left.

Miles and Directions

0.0   Begin at the Mavell Road parking area. (GPS: N33 50.503' / W84 31.037')

0.7 Cross the bridge.

2.3 Cross the bridge over the East-West Connector, after which a side trail descends to Heritage Park. (GPS: N33 51.035' / W84 33.339')

3.0 Continue through the Hurt Road Tunnel.

4.2 End your hike on Floyd Road at the Silver Comet Depot store and parking area. (GPS: N33 50.822' / W84 35.140')

5 Chattahoochee River National Recreation Area: Cochran Shoals Unit

With its popular 3.1-mile fitness trail along the river and floodplain, Cochran Shoals is the Chattahoochee River National Recreation Area's busiest unit (the parking area quickly fills on weekends). Beyond the fitness trail, challenging hiking paths climb into the surrounding hills. One path, the Scribner Trail, links Cochran Shoals with the adjacent Sope Creek Unit of the park.

Distance: 5.5-mile interconnected loop

Approximate hiking time: 2–3 hours

Elevation gain/loss: 164 feet

Trail surface: Fine gravel, boardwalks, compact dirt, and sandy floodplain

Difficulty: Moderate due to distance and terrain

Best Season: All year

Other trail users: Bicyclists

Canine compatibility: Leashed dogs permitted

Land status: National Park Service

Fees and permits: Daily pass/annual pass

Schedule: Open daily, dawn to dusk

Maps: *USGS Sandy Springs.* Maps also available from the park Web site.

Trail contacts: Chattahoochee River National Recreation Area, 1978 Island Ford Pkwy., Atlanta 30350; (678) 538-1200; www.nps.gov/chat

Finding the trailhead: From I-285, exit on Northside Drive/New Northside Drive (exit 22). At the exit travel north on Interstate Parkway North. The parkway curves to the left (west) and descends first to the Powers Island parking area, then across the river to the Cochran Shoals parking area. There is a satellite parking area on Columns Drive at the north end of the Cochran Shoals Unit. It may

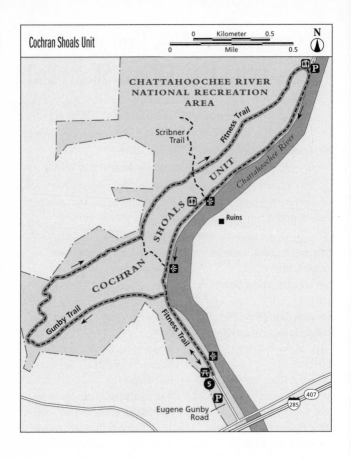

Kilometer

Mile

N

CHATTAHOOCHEE RIVER
NATIONAL RECREATION
AREA

Fitness Trail

Scribner
Trail

COCHRAN SHOALS UNIT

Chattahoochee River

Ruins

Gunby Trail

Fitness Trail

5

P

Eugene Gunby
Road

407
285

be reached by exiting I-285 at Riverside Drive (exit 24) and traveling north for 2.4 miles to Johnson Ferry Road. Turn left (north), crossing the Chattahoochee River past the CRNRA Johnson Ferry Unit, and turn left (south) on Columns Drive at 1.0 mile. The road winds through the Johnson Ferry Unit before reaching a parking area for Cochran Shoals at 2.6 miles. **GPS:** N33 54.113' / W84 26.411'

The Hike

Beginning from the Cochran Shoals parking lot, pass the information board, and walk along the wide, gravel fitness trail that follows the river. At 0.5 mile bear left and follow the Gunby Trail over a boardwalk, then through a wetland area. Beyond the boardwalk continue straight through a signed intersection, as the footpath ascends through a power line corridor. Cross and continue climbing toward the park boundary near an office building at 1.3 miles.

The trail bends right and ascends a short distance before turning right again as it closes the loop. After a short distance the path reaches a ridgeline before beginning a gentle descent to a signed intersection. Turn left and descend to a bottomland creek bed. You will cross a footbridge over a stream at 1.8 miles and bend right. Cross a second bridge as the path winds through a lowland area before rejoining the fitness trail at 2.4 miles.

Turn left, cross a footbridge, and pass two side trails. The trail to the left leads into the surrounding hills while the path to the right leads to a comfort station and a return to the parking area. At 2.8 miles the Scribner Trail, connecting with the Sope Creek Unit, exits to the left. Continue straight, reaching the Columns Drive entrance to the park at 3.5 miles. Bear right and begin the return loop toward the starting point. At 4.4 miles you will pass a short path to a river observation deck before crossing a footbridge by a comfort station. Continue on the fitness trail, returning to the parking area at 5.5 miles.

Miles and Directions

0.0 Begin the hike at the parking area by the information kiosk and picnic tables. (GPS: N33 54.113' / W84 26.411')

0.5 Turn left on the Gunby Trail. (GPS: N33 54.320' / W84 26.562')

0.7 Continue straight on the dirt path.

1.3 The trail bends right at the park boundary near a large office building.

1.8 Cross a footbridge and turn right.

2.4 Rejoin the Cochran Shoals Fitness Trail and turn left. (GPS: N33 54.473' / W84 27.387')

2.8 Continue straight, past the intersection with the Scribner Trail.

3.5 From the Columns Drive entrance, turn right on the return loop. (GPS: N33 55.268' / W84 26.390')

4.4 On the left is a river observation deck. A short distance ahead is a comfort station and rest area.

5.5 Arrive back at the Cochran Shoals parking area.

6 Kennesaw Mountain National Battlefield Park: Summit–Pigeon Hill Loop Trail

The 2,888-acre Kennesaw Mountain National Battlefield Park preserves the site of battles fought between Union and Confederate Armies from June 22 to July 2, 1864. In addition to restored fortifications, Kennesaw Mountain and surrounding woodlands are important wildlife habitats. The mountain, a landmark on the Eastern migratory flyway, is designated an Important Bird Area (IBA) along the southern edge of the Blue Ridge Mountains. Pause before or after your hike to view exhibits in the visitor center and learn about park interpretive programs.

Distance: 5.8-mile loop trail
Approximate hiking time: 3–4 hours
Difficulty: More challenging due to distance and terrain
Elevation gain/loss: 696 feet
Trail surface: Mix of compacted soil, asphalt, and gravel
Best season: All year
Canine compatibility: Leashed dogs permitted
Fees and permits: None

Schedule: Park trails open daily from dawn to dusk; visitor center open daily 8:30 a.m.–5 p.m., later in summer
Maps: *USGS Marietta.* Maps also available from the visitor center and at the park Web site.
Trail contacts: Kennesaw Mountain National Battlefield Park, 900 Kennesaw Mountain Dr., Kennesaw 30152; (770) 427-4686; www.nps.gov/kemo

Finding the trailhead: From Atlanta, travel north on I-75 to Barrett Parkway (exit 263). Turn left (west) and drive 3.1 miles to Old US 41, then turn left (east). After 1.3 miles turn right (south) on

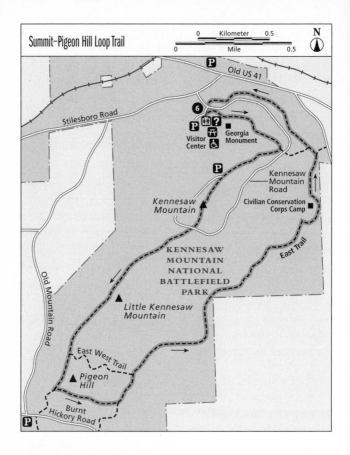

Stilesboro Road. The park entrance will be immediately on the left. There is also a small satellite parking area on Burnt Hickory Road.
GPS: N33 58.982' / W84 34.722'

The Hike

The trail begins across the summit or mountain road behind

the visitor center. The path gradually ascends on a series of switchbacks to an intersection with the old, gravel summit road, bending right and continuing along the old road before ascending, at times steeply, to the Kennesaw Mountain summit parking area. It follows the sidewalk and stone steps to a large observation deck before climbing, on an asphalt surface, past restored artillery fortifications to a rock outcrop on the mountain summit at 1.0 mile.

The trail then steeply descends along a rocky path to a crossing of the summit road. On the opposite side follow steps down to a path across a saddle before climbing to the wooded summit of Little Kennesaw Mountain, site of a reconstruction of the Rebels' Fort McBride, at 1.9 miles. Pause here to read the dramatic story of how Rebels hauled heavy cannons by hand up the steep slopes.

The trail continues on a steep descent along rock- and root-studded slopes, following a series of long switchbacks to level, heavily wooded terrain. Pass an intersection marked EAST WEST TRAIL, before entering an area of large boulders and rock outcrops dubbed Pigeon Hill. From this vantage point it is easy to see why the Rebels considered this a superb defensive position. Descend along exposed rocks past an intersection, continuing a short distance to a sign noting the scene of bitter fighting between Missouri soldiers serving the North and South. Retrace your steps and turn right at the intersection. Follow this path to the East Trail at 2.7 miles.

Turn left on the East Trail, following the route of a service road built by the Civilian Conservation Corps (CCC) in the 1930s (Corps enrollees developed the first park facilities and trails). At 4.7 miles a side path leads to the site of the CCC camp, with its traces of old buildings and parade ground still in evidence. Beyond the camp, the trail forks left, then a short distance ahead, it forks again. Bear right to return to the visitor center at 5.8 miles.

Miles and Directions

0.0 The trail begins across the summit road south of the visitor center. (GPS: N33 58.982' / W84 34.722')

0.2 The trail bears right on to the old park service summit road.

0.4 From the old road, the trail bends right and ascends.

0.8 Reach the summit parking area and shuttle bus stop. Follow the sidewalk to the observation platform.

1.0 At the summit of Kennesaw Mountain is a USGS survey marker at 1,793 feet. (GPS: N33 58.582' / W84 34.752')

1.6 Begin a steady ascent to Little Kennesaw Mountain.

1.9 At the summit of Little Kennesaw Mountain is a reconstruction of Fort McBride.

2.5 Continue straight at the intersection with the East West Trail (a shortcut to the visitor center).

2.7 Follow the loop trail to the left toward the East Trail. (GPS: N33 57.871' / W84 35.530')

3.0 Turn left toward the visitor center at the East (Cheatham Hill) Trail intersection.

4.7 The trail reaches a meadow and the site of a CCC camp. Note the scattered ruins of camp structures.

4.8 Take the left fork to the visitor center.

5.1 Follow the right-hand path to a field east of Summit Road.

5.8 Pass a stand of trees to reach the visitor center.

7 Pickett's Mill Battlefield State Historic Site

In reports from the Union Army's 1864 march into Georgia, General William T. Sherman barely mentioned the May 27 fighting at Pickett's Mill. The likely reason is that, among a string of victories, this battle was a stunning defeat. After the war the site remained virtually unchanged and is among the nation's best preserved Civil War battlefields. Noted short-story writer Ambrose Bierce was a young Union lieutenant at Pickett's Mill. The dark nature of his writing has been attributed to his war experiences. His eyewitness account of the battle, "The Crime at Pickett's Mill," offers a sobering picture of war's brutality.

Distance: 4.1-mile interconnecting loops

Approximate hiking time: 2–3 hours

Difficulty: Easy to moderate due to rolling terrain and distance

Elevation gain/loss: 175 feet

Trail surface: Compacted soil

Best seasons: Spring and fall

Canine compatibility: Leashed dogs permitted

Fees and permits: Daily parking fee or annual pass

Schedule: 9 a.m.–5 p.m. Thur-Sat; closed Sun–Wed (except holidays)

Maps: USGS Dallas, Georgia. Trail guides also available for purchase at the visitor center.

Trail contacts: Pickett's Mill Battlefield State Historic Site, 4432 Mount Tabor Church Rd., Dallas, GA 30157; (770) 443-7850; www.gastateparks.org

Finding the trailhead: From Atlanta, drive north on I-75 to GA 92 (exit 277). Turn left (south) and follow GA 92 south for 4.1 miles to US 41 and turn right (north). In 1.9 miles turn left (south) on the continuation of GA 92 and drive 4.0 miles to the GA 92–GA 381

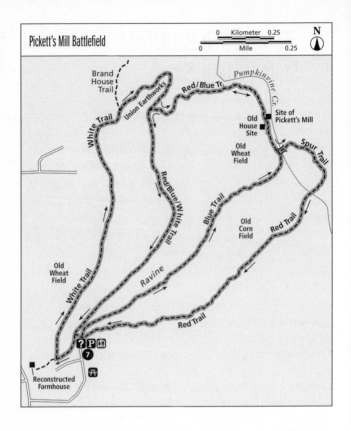

Pickett's Mill Battlefield

0 Kilometer 0.25
0 Mile 0.25

N

Brand House Trail

Red/Blue Tr.

Pumpkinvine Cr.

White Trail

Union Earthworks

Old House Site

Site of Pickett's Mill

Old Wheat Field

Spur Trail

Red/Blue/White Trail

Blue Trail

Old Corn Field

Red Trail

Old Wheat Field

White Trail

Ravine

Red Trail

? P

7

Reconstructed Farmhouse

(Dallas-Acworth Highway) split. Continue straight on GA 381 for 2.3 miles to Mount Tabor Church Road. Turn right (east) and travel 1.0 mile to the park entrance on the right. **GPS:** N33 58.437' / W84 45.548'

The Hike

From the rear of the visitor center, descend steps and turn left on the Blue Trail. At 0.1 mile bear right on the White

Trail (an old farm road) and descend past a meadow that was a wheat field during the Civil War. The path forks left at 0.3 mile and you will meander through a wooded area to the intersection of the Brand House Trail. Bear right and continue past fading remains of Union earthworks.

Follow the path as it descends to the intersection of the Red, Blue, and White Trails. Turn left on the Red/Blue Trail and continue down a wooded slope, passing another meadow (also once a wheat field). At 1.1 miles you will reach Pumpkinvine Creek (once known as Pickett's Mill Creek) and the site of Pickett's Mill. Badly damaged during the Civil War battle at Pickett's Mill, stone foundations are all that remain of the structure. Ascend past the site of the long-vanished miller's home and well.

At 1.4 miles turn left on the Red Trail and descend to a bridge over the creek. Ascend through wooded hills, crossing a second bridge before reaching a meadow (a corn-field back in 1864). Bear right and continue along wooded slopes, reaching a left turn on the Red Trail at 2.3 miles.

As you approach the visitor center on the Red Trail, turn right on the Blue Trail and follow the edge of a steep ravine that was the site of the battle's fiercest fighting. As you walk above, glance downward and imagine Rebel soldiers pouring deadly fire into the Union troops below. After retracing your steps on the combined Red/Blue Trail, past the mill site and the wheat field, you will reach the intersection with the Red/Blue/White Trail at 3.3 miles.

Turn left and descend on the combined trail as it meanders along the floor of a narrow valley west of the ravine where thousands of blue-clad soldiers were trapped during the Civil War. Ascend to the ridge above at 3.9 miles and turn left to return to the starting point at 4.1 miles. You may also turn right to retrace your steps past the White Trail to follow the old Leverett Farm Road to see a reconstructed antebellum farmhouse (0.3-mile round-trip).

Miles and Directions

0.0 From the deck behind the visitor center, turn left and hike to the White Trail. (GPS: N33 58.437' / W84 45.548')

0.1 Bear right on the White Trail.

0.3 The trail forks left from the old road.

0.7 Past the Union earthworks, reach the Red/Blue/White Trails intersection. (GPS: N33 58.872' / W84 45.405')

1.1 The site of Pickett's Mill is adjacent to Pumpkinvine Creek.

1.4 Turn left on the Red Trail.

2.3 At the edge of the meadow (cornfield), bear left along the Red Trail.

2.6 Turn right on the Blue Trail and follow the ravine.

3.3 Descend into the ravine on the Red/Blue/White Trail.

3.9 Ascend to the ridge and turn left.

4.1 When you reach the visitor center, take time to view the exhibits.

8 Red Top Mountain State Park: Homestead and Sweetgum Trails

Nestled on a 1,950-acre Allatoona Lake peninsula, Red Top Mountain is among Georgia's most popular state parks. Centuries ago these hills were home to Paleo-Indians who built mysterious mounds, which are now preserved at nearby Etowah Mounds State Historic Site. After the Cherokee removal on the Trail of Tears in the 1830s, the hills were mined for their rich iron ore. The mines were destroyed during the Civil War, but remnants may still be seen at nearby Cooper Furnace Park. Following creation of Allatoona Lake by the Corps of Engineers in the 1950s, the state set aside this land for the park.

Distance: 6.25-mile figure-8 trail
Approximate hiking time: 3 hours
Difficulty: Moderate due to terrain and distance
Elevation gain/loss: 179 feet
Trail surface: Compacted soil
Best season: All year
Canine compatibility: Leashed dogs permitted
Fees and permits: Daily parking fee (free Wed) or annual pass
Schedule: Daily 7 a.m.–10 p.m.
Maps: *USGS Allatoona Dam.* Maps also available in the Trading Post, the Lodge, and at the park Web site.
Trail contacts: Red Top Mountain State Park, 50 Lodge Rd., Cartersville 30121; (770) 975-0055; www.gastateparks.org

Finding the trailhead: From Atlanta, drive north on I-75 to Red Top Mountain Road (exit 285). Turn right (east) and drive 1.8 miles to Marina Road. Turn left (north) and travel 0.7 mile to Lodge Road. Turn right (east) and travel a short distance to the lodge parking area and hike starting point. **GPS:** N34 09.252' / W84 42.165'

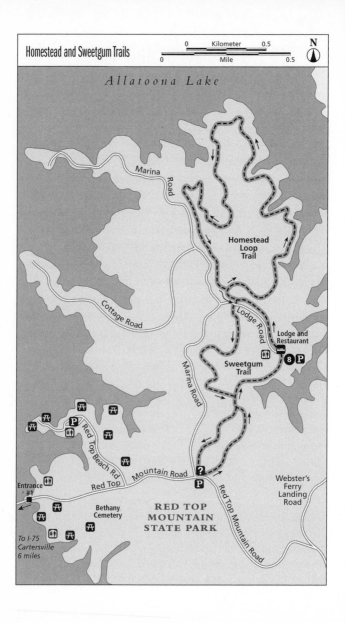

Homestead and Sweetgum Trails

Kilometer 0
0.5

Mile 0
0.5

N

Allatoona Lake

Marina Road

Homestead Loop Trail

Cottage Road

Lodge Road

Lodge and Restaurant

8 P

Sweetgum Trail

Marina Road

?

P

Red Top Beach Rd

Mountain Road

Red Top

Entrance #1

Bethany Cemetery

RED TOP MOUNTAIN STATE PARK

Red Top Mountain Road

Webster's Ferry Landing Road

To I-75 Cartersville 6 miles

The Hike

This hike begins at the Red Top Mountain Lodge, located near the intersection of the Homestead and Sweetgum Trails. Walk north from the lodge parking area to a sign for the Sweetgum (red blaze) Trail. A short distance ahead the 0.5-mile White Tail Nature Trail (white blaze) exits right to a scenic lake overlook. The red blazes lead to an intersection with the Homestead Trail (yellow blaze) at 0.4 mile.

Follow the yellow blazes to the right and descend to a trail fork. Turn right, hiking through a lowland area as the trail bends left and then right, reaching a lake cove at 0.7 mile. Ascend a ridge before hiking downward to a lake viewpoint at 1.1 miles. The trail then crosses slopes above the lake on a series of switchbacks.

At 2.1 miles the path bends left, away from the water, passing an unblazed side trail on the right. At 2.8 miles bend right and continue ascending along switchbacks. You will reach a ridge at 3.0 miles where the path turns right and begins a gentle downward course. Close the loop at 3.7 miles and retrace your steps to the entrance road. At this point you may continue the hike or return to the lodge.

After crossing the road follow the combined Homestead and Sweetgum Trails on a gentle descent to a bridge at 3.9 miles. At the trail fork, follow the yellow trail to the right as it climbs to a ridge. The path bends left, descending to rejoin the Sweetgum Trail. Bear right, through bottomland, to an intersection at 4.4 miles, following the yellow blazes to the hills above a creek. The trail follows a rolling course below Marina Road, gently descending to bottomlands before climbing to the park's Trading Post (visitor center) at 5.0 miles.

To return to the lodge, descend on the red-blazed trail by the tennis courts to an intersection with the 0.7-mile Visitor Center Loop Trail (green blaze). Turn left on the Sweetgum Trail, continuing down to a lowland area and across a shallow creek on footbridges. Reach the merge of the Sweetgum and Homestead Trails at 5.8 miles and follow the red blazes to the right. Gently ascend along the lake's edge, passing the intersection with the short 0.7-mile Lakeside Trail (black blaze). Return to the lodge parking area at 6.2 miles.

Miles and Directions

0.0 Begin at the Sweetgum Trail sign north of the Red Top Mountain Lodge. (GPS: N34 09.252' / W84 42.165')

0.4 Turn right at the intersection with the Homestead Trail.

0.8 The trail bends to the left above Allatoona Lake.

1.1 Reach a bench with a lake view.

2.1 The trail ascends away from the lake.

2.8 Bend right and continue ascending along switchbacks.

3.0 After steadily ascending, the trail bends right.

3.7 Cross the entrance road on the combined Homestead and Sweetgum Trails. (GPS: N34 09.455' / W84 42.528')

3.9 Arrive at a bridge.

4.4 At the fork follow the Homestead Trail to the right.

4.6 When the trails rejoin, remain on the Homestead Trail.

5.0 Reach the Trading Post. (GPS: N34 08.881' / W84 42.398')

5.8 Continue on the Sweetgum Trail when the paths fork.

6.25 Exit the woods south of the Red Top Mountain Lodge.

9 Chattahoochee Nature Center

The 127-acre Chattahoochee Nature Center (CNC) preserves habitats along the Chattahoochee River. The family-
oriented center offers more than 3 miles of marked trails,
ponds and streams for observing native wildlife, exhibits and
classrooms, wild-animal rescue and recovery services, and
educational programs for all ages. The multimillion-dollar
Interpretive Center for the Chattahoochee River Watershed
opened in June 2009.

Distance: 2.9 miles of
interconnected loops
Approximate hiking time: 2 hours
Difficulty: Moderate with some
steep hills
Elevation gain/loss: 118 feet
Trail surface: Compacted soil,
boardwalk, and pavement
Best Season: All year
Canine compatibility: Dogs
prohibited
Fees and permits: Admission fee.
Annual memberships available.

Schedule: 9 a.m.–5 p.m. Mon-
Sat, noon–5 p.m. Sun
Maps: *USGS Mountain Park.*
Maps also available from the
nature center's Web site. Indi-
vidual trail maps with numbered
stops are also available at the
center.
Trail contacts: Chattahoochee
Nature Center, 9135 Willeo Rd.,
Roswell 30075; (770) 992-
2055; www.chattnaturecenter.org

Finding the trailhead: From Atlanta, drive north on GA 400 to
Northridge Road (exit 6). Exit and remain in the right lane. Cross the
bridge and turn right (north) at the traffic light on Dunwoody Place.
Travel north for 1.2 miles to Roswell Road. Turn right (north) and
drive 0.7 mile, across the Chattahoochee River, and turn left (west)
on Azalea Drive. Drive 1.8 miles to Willeo Road. Turn left (south)
on Willeo and travel 1.5 miles to the Chattahoochee Nature Center
entrance drive on the right. The trails begin behind the nature center
administration building. **GPS:** N34 0.270' / W84 22.950'

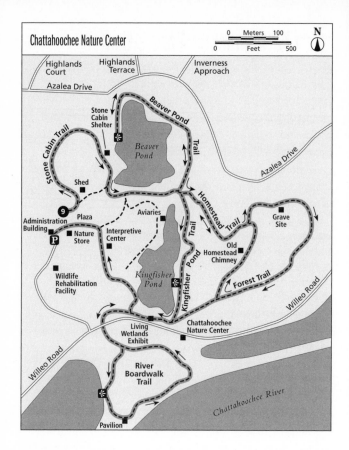

The Hike

The hike begins in the plaza behind the Chattahoochee Nature Center administration building. Turn left and follow the path west of the maintenance building. At a trail fork bear right to the Stone Cabin Trail (yellow blaze). Follow the trail across a wooded ridge and down to a footbridge over a stream. You will cross and climb another ridge before descending to Beaver Pond. Turn right and pass the Stone Cabin Shelter before descending to the intersection with the Beaver Pond Trail (green blaze) at 0.3 mile.

Turn left on the green-blazed trail and descend to an intersection with the paved Butterfly Garden Trail that winds back to the plaza. Continue straight, past a pond overlook and across an earthen dam to a T-intersection at 0.5 mile. Bear left on the Beaver Pond Trail and enjoy excellent vantage points for observing waterfowl and wildlife. The trail terminates at a pond overlook at 0.7 mile.

Retrace your steps to the dam and continue straight on the Kingfisher Pond Trail (blue blaze). Cross a bridge and turn left at a trail intersection on the Homestead Trail (orange blaze). You will climb, sometimes steeply, to a rest area with a bench at 1.2 miles. Turn left on the Forest Trail (red blaze) and continue up a short distance to the highest point on the CNC property. Nearby is the unmarked grave of Charles Kelpen, whose family owned this land before the Civil War. In 1863 Kelpen left his job at the nearby Roswell Mill to join the Confederate Army and died from disease at an Augusta, Georgia, hospital in 1864.

Follow the slope on a long descent through second-growth forest to an intersection with the Homestead Trail at 1.5 miles. Turn right and climb steadily, past the remnants of a 1940s vacation cottage, before reaching the Forest Trail intersection. Retrace your steps down to the Kingfisher Pond Trail at 1.8 miles. Turn left and follow the blue-blazed path along Kingfisher Pond. At 2.0 miles you will reach an outdoor classroom area and pond overlook platform with a viewing scope for spotting and identification of waterfowl.

Soon you will turn right on a paved path with exhibits that describe different wetland habitats. From the paved trail, turn left and carefully cross Willeo Road to the River Boardwalk Trail (purple blaze) at 2.2 miles. Follow the boardwalk through marsh habitats to an overlook platform at 2.4 miles. Continue on the loop, past a shelter and several panoramic viewpoints of the Chattahoochee River (look for evidence of beaver dams as you walk). The path closes the loop at 2.7 miles before recrossing Willeo Road. Follow the path to the left and ascend to the Interpretive Center.

Miles and Directions

0.0 Turn left from the plaza behind the nature store. (GPS: N34 0.270' / W84 22.950')

0.1 Bear right to Stone Cabin Trail.

0.2 Reach the stone cabin shelter.

0.5 Cross the earthen dam and turn left at the intersection on Beaver Pond Trail. (GPS: N34 0.300' / W84 22.827')

0.7 Reach the pond overlook at end of Beaver Pond Trail. Retrace your steps back to the Kingfisher Pond Trail intersection.

1.1 Turn left and begin your ascent on the Homestead Trail.

1.2 Reach an intersection with the Forest Trail on the left. (GPS: N34 0.270' / W84 22.727')

1.5 Turn right and ascend on Homestead Trail. (GPS: N34 0.168' / W84 22.821')

1.6 Pass remnants of an old cabin.

1.8 After your descent on Homestead Trail, turn left on Kingfisher Pond Trail.

2.0 Pause at the outdoor classroom and pond overlook.

2.2 After crossing Willeo Road, reach the River Boardwalk Trail.

2.4 Pause at the marsh and river overlook platform. (GPS: N34 0.063' / W84 22.921')

2.7 Recross Willeo Road.

2.9 Arrive at the Interpretive Center.

10 Chattahoochee River National Recreation Area: Island Ford Unit

When President Jimmy Carter created the Chattahoochee River National Recreation Area in 1978, this site, including the former retreat of Judge Samuel Hewlett (ca. 1930s), was selected as headquarters. Today the log and stone structure is the park's visitor center.

Nineteenth-century pioneers, settling this area after removal of the Cherokee on the Trail of Tears, sought shallow fords to bring their families across the river. One such site was here at Island Ford. Today the rocky shoals attract fly-fishers, while hikers trek along the banks and through the surrounding hills.

Distance: 2.8-mile hike of interconnecting loops
Approximate hiking time: 2 hours
Elevation gain/loss: 190 feet
Trail surface: Mix of compact soil and sandy floodplain
Difficulty: Moderate due to distance and terrain
Season: All year
Canine compatibility: Leashed dogs permitted

Fees and permits: Daily or annual pass
Schedule: Park open daily, dawn to dark; visitor center open daily 9 a.m.–5 p.m.
Maps: *USGS Chamblee.* Maps also available from park Web site.
Trail contacts: Chattahoochee River National Recreation Area, 1978 Island Ford Pkwy., Atlanta 30350; (678) 538-1200; www .nps.gov/chat

Finding the trailhead: Travel north on GA 400 to Northridge Road (exit 6). Cross the bridge, remaining in the right lane, and turn right (north) at the first traffic light on Dunwoody Place. Drive north for

0.6 mile and turn right (east) on Roberts Drive. Travel for 0.7 mile, crossing beneath GA 400, to Island Ford Parkway. Turn right (north) and follow the parkway for 1.0 mile, turning left (east) into the visitor center parking area. **GPS:** N33 59.232' / W84 19.497'

The Hike

This is a path of rugged and exceptional scenic beauty. Begin at the visitor center by descending steps on the right to the floodplain trail near a boat ramp and recreation field. Turn left, following the path along the river to a footbridge at 0.2 mile. Continue straight (the path to the left returns to the parking lot) and enjoy views of the Chattahoochee as it flows over rocky shoals. Ahead at 0.5 mile is a signed intersection by a large overhanging rock (the trail to the left returns to the visitor center). Continue along the river, crossing a footbridge and past another large rock outcrop. You will reach another signed intersection at 0.7 mile where the path to the left shortens the loop. Proceed straight, past another upland trail, before bearing west at 0.8 mile and ascending above Beech Creek.

The path climbs the wooded slopes before crossing a bridge over a stream and past a trail that leads to a parking area. A short distance ahead, reach a trail junction just below a ridge. At the trail marker, bend right to continue the loop path (the trail to the left descends to the river), and cross a ridge with a descent of the far slope. Follow the path downward, crossing Summerbrook Creek on rocks, before rejoining the river trail at 1.8 miles. Turn right, retracing your steps for 0.3 mile before ascending the trail to the right to a parking area. Cross the road and reenter the woods as the path follows the shore of a small pond. Cross the footbridge over a stream at 2.3 miles and climb steps as the trail

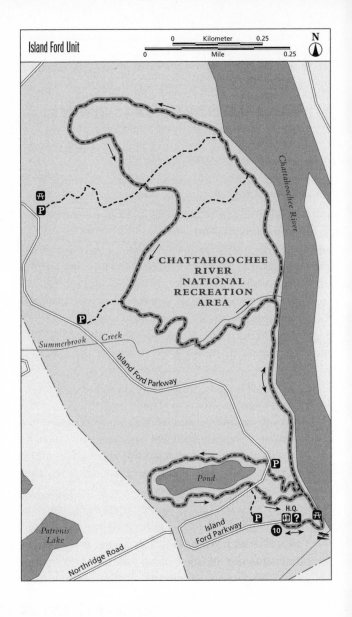

follows the slope above the water. Continue east and close the loop around the pond.

Recross the road and follow another set of steps past a trail marker. Reenter the woods, descending past a stream to the river trail. Note the stonework and an old pump house beside the visitor center. Reach the river at 2.8 miles and turn right, ascending past a picnic shelter to the starting point.

Miles and Directions

0.0 Descend steps to the right of the visitor center. (GPS: N33 59.232' / W84 19.497')

0.5 Pass a large rock outcrop by a signed intersection. (GPS: N33 59.505' / W84 19.521')

0.9 Ascend away from the water.

1.1 Pass a side trail to a parking lot.

1.8 Rejoin the river trail.

2.2 Follow the shore of the small pond.

2.5 Cross the entrance road.

2.6 Return to the river.

2.8 Arrive back at the visitor center.

11 Laurel Ridge Trail on Lake Sidney Lanier

Nestled in the Appalachian foothills adjacent to Lake Lanier's Buford Dam, Laurel Ridge Trail offers a glimpse of the landscape as it appeared before the lake was completed by the Corps of Engineers in 1957. From the trail section below the dam, a bridge crosses the Chattahoochee River to Bowman's Island, a unit of the Chattahoochee River National Recreation Area. The lake is named for Georgia-born poet Sidney Lanier, best known for his works "The Song of the Chattahoochee," "Sunrise," and "The Marshes of Glynn."

Distance: 3.8-mile loop trail

Approximate hiking time: 3 hours

Difficulty: Moderate due to terrain

Elevation gain/loss: 256 feet

Trail surface: Compacted soil, with some pavement, steps, and wooden boardwalks

Best seasons: Spring and fall

Canine compatibility: Dogs not permitted

Fees and permits: Free

Schedule: Trails open daily during daylight hours. Park hours are posted at the entrance.

Maps: *USGS Buford Dam.* Trail map also available from the Corps of Engineers Web site.

Trail contacts: U.S. Army Corps of Engineers, Lake Lanier Management Office, 1050 Buford Dam Rd., Buford 30518; (770) 945-9531; http://lanier.sam. usace.army.mil

Special considerations: Sirens warn of pending water releases from the dam when the river may rise by as much as 11 feet.

Finding the trailhead: From Atlanta, travel north on I-85 to Lawrenceville-Suwanee Road/GA 317 (exit 111). Turn left (west) at the ramp and follow GA 317 for 2.1 miles to Buford Highway/ US 23. Continue straight on Suwanee-Buford Dam Road (the name will change to Suwanee Dam Road) for 7.4 miles. Turn left (west) on Buford Dam Road for 0.4 mile and turn right (north) into the Lower Overlook Park parking area.

From GA 400, travel east on Buford Highway/GA 20 (exit 14) to Market Place Boulevard and turn left (north). Drive 0.6 mile and turn right (east) on Buford Dam Road. Travel 5.2 miles, across Buford Dam, and turn left (north) to the Lower Overlook Park parking area. **GPS:** N34 09.536' / W84 04.212'

The Hike

From Lower Overlook Park, follow the concrete path behind a comfort station through a shallow ravine. Cross Buford Dam Road and climb to the right past Upper Overlook Park. Glance to the right for a panoramic view of Buford Dam before descending to a second overlook platform. Follow steep steps down to Power House Road at 0.6 mile. Cross and continue descending to the Chattahoochee River. Follow the wooden bridge along the floodplain. A short distance ahead a boardwalk exits to the right and crosses the river to Bowman's Island's Lower Pool Park and boat ramp. Several vantage points offer good views of the 2,360-foot-long dam that rises nearly 200 feet above the river.

At 0.9 mile the trail bends sharply left and ascends to the surrounding woodlands. The climb is gradual to a footbridge over a stream, then it steepens on switchbacks, reaching Buford Dam Road at 1.5 miles. Cross and descend steps to reenter an upland forest. Continue down, crossing a power line corridor, before dropping more steeply on the far side. The trail follows a boardwalk through fern-filled wetlands before crossing a service road at 2.2 miles. A short distance ahead, the trail bends right through Buford Dam Park. Follow trail signs along the sidewalk, turning left and descend-

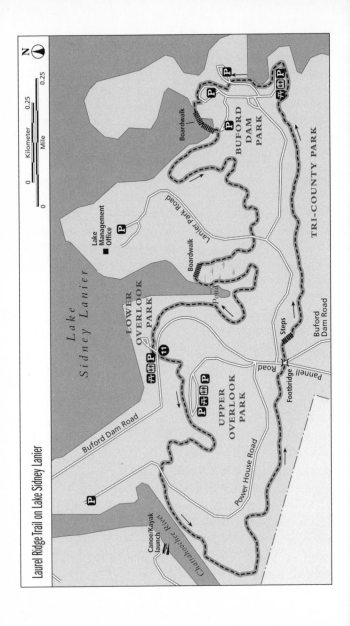

ing past two group shelters above the lake. Continue down a short switchback, past a side trail to an overlook, before crossing a cove on an elevated footbridge.

The trail ascends to the right, past a picnic area at 2.7 miles. Follow the signed trail to the left, past a comfort station, then descend on steps to the right, crossing an elevated boardwalk to the left. After a steep ascent past a parking area, the trail reenters the woods on a pine-shaded ridge with good lake views. Bear left and descend on switchbacks to Lanier Park Road at 3.2 miles. Cross and continue down to a series of boardwalks meandering through a wetlands area.

The path bends sharply left along a small pond before ascending again. After a moderate climb, the trail follows the slope below Buford Dam Road to the starting point at 3.8 miles.

Miles and Directions

0.0 Begin at the Lower Overlook Park parking area east of Buford Dam. (GPS: N34 09.536' / W84 04.212')

0.6 Cross Power House Road.

0.9 Ascend away from the river. (GPS: N34 09.347' / W84 04.710')

1.4 A footbridge crosses the stream.

1.5 Cross Buford Dam Road and descend the steps.

2.2 The boardwalk crosses a wetland area.

2.3 Turn right to enter Buford Dam Park. (GPS: N34 09.360' / W84 03.670')

2.7 Reach a picnic and playground area.

3.2 Cross Lanier Park Road and descend on steps to a wetlands area with boardwalks. (GPS: N34 09.345' / W84 04.030')

3.8 After a steady climb, return to the starting point.

12 Sawnee Mountain Preserve

The preserve, located north of Cumming, features a 4-mile network of foot trails along the slopes of 1,963-foot Sawnee Mountain (named for a Cherokee chief). The exposed rocks just below the summit, dubbed Indian Seats, offer spectacular vistas. In addition to trekking, enthusiasts may rock climb and rappel (by permit) and enjoy outdoor educational programs. This hike begins from the Environmental Learning Center at the preserve's northern entrance. As you hike, watch for evidence of early-twentieth-century gold mining. Future plans will expand the park with additional trails on the west side of Bettis-Tribble Gap Road.

Distance: 4.4-mile lollipop
Approximate hiking time: 2 hours
Difficulty: Moderate due to terrain
Elevation gain/loss: 597 feet
Trail surface: Compacted soil
Best season: All year
Canine compatibility: Dogs are prohibited
Fees and permits: Free
Schedule: Park open daily 8 a.m. to dark. Environmental Learning Center open 8:30 a.m.–5 p.m. Mon–Fri, 10 a.m.–5 p.m. Sat, 1 p.m.–5 p.m. Sun (seasonally).
Maps: *USGS Cumming*. Maps also available at the park and on the Forsyth County Web site.
Trail contacts: Forsyth County Parks and Recreation Department, P.O. Box 2417, Cumming, GA 30040; (770) 781-2215; www.forsythco.com

Finding the trailhead: From Atlanta, travel north on GA 400 to Bald Ridge Marina Road (exit 15). Travel west 1.2 miles to downtown Cumming and turn right (north) on Tribble Gap Road (it soon changes to Bettis-Tribble Gap Road). At 3.0 miles you will see the southern entrance to Sawnee Mountain Reserve on the right. Continue straight for 1.0 mile to Spot Road and turn right. The preserve's northern entrance will be 0.3 mile ahead on the right at 4075 Spot Rd. **GPS:** N34 15.313' / W84 08.337'

The Hike

From the Environmental Learning Center, follow the access trail past information boards to the Tree Canopy Classroom (Tree House) at 0.3 mile. A short distance ahead you will turn right at the Laurel Trail intersection. Ascend steadily along the wooded slope before beginning your descent at 0.8 mile toward the south entrance. At 1.3 miles you will pass a short side trail on the left that leads to an old mine tunnel (gated). A few paces beyond, the Laurel Trail climbs away to the left. Continue straight for 0.2 mile to the activity area, which features picnic pavilions, a playground, an amphitheater, a comfort station, and parking.

Continue east on the Indian Seats Trail as it crosses a creek bottom with fading evidence of mining pits, before climbing toward the mountain summit. At 1.9 miles pass the Yucca Trail on the left and continue ascending on long switchbacks, reaching Indian Seats at 2.3 miles. Pause to read the descriptive marker before trekking a short distance to the right to an overlook platform with a panoramic view northward to the Blue Ridge Mountains. Retrace your steps to rejoin the Indian Seats Trail as it gently descends westward.

At 3.0 miles rejoin the Laurel Trail and continue straight on a steep descent through stands of mountain laurel. The grade becomes less steep as the path follows long switchbacks, reaching the lower Laurel Trail intersection at 3.7 miles. Continue straight on the access trail to the Environmental Learning Center at 4.4 miles.

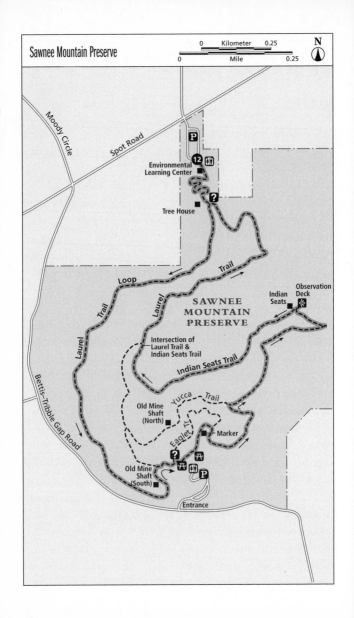

Miles and Directions

0.0 Follow the access trail behind the Environmental Learning Center. (GPS: N34 15.313' / W84 08.337')

0.4 Pass the Tree Canopy Classroom and turn right on lower Laurel Trail.

0.8 Begin the descent toward the south entrance of the park.

1.4 Continue straight where the Laurel Trail exits to the left.

1.5 Reach the south entrance area. (GPS: N34 14.702' / W84 08.334')

1.9 Climb past the Yucca Trail intersection.

2.3 Enjoy the panoramic views from Indian Seats. (GPS: N34 15.012' / W84 08.107')

3.0 Rejoin the Laurel Trail and continue the descent.

3.7 Retrace your steps on the access trail.

4.4 Arrive back at the Environmental Learning Center.

13 State Botanical Garden of Georgia

Established by the University of Georgia in 1968, the 313-acre gardens complex includes a glass-enclosed conservatory and visitor center, the stone and timber Day Chapel, the Callaway classroom building, and the Garden Club of Georgia headquarters. In addition to paths through gardens of native and exotic plants and herbs, the garden features more than 5 miles of trails in surrounding forests, wetlands, and floodplains of the Middle Oconee River. The State Botanical Garden serves as a "living laboratory" for university instruction and research, as well as a destination for hikers, gardening buffs, and wildlife-watchers.

Distance: 4.9-mile interconnected loop

Approximate hiking time: 3 hours

Elevation gain/loss: 166 feet

Trail surface: Compact soil, gravel, short paved sections

Difficulty: Moderate

Season: All year

Canine compatibility: Dogs prohibited

Fees and permits: Free (donations encouraged and memberships available)

Schedule: Gardens open daily 8 a.m.–6 p.m. (8 p.m. in summer); visitor center and conservatory open 9 a.m.–4:30 p.m. Tues–Sat, 11:30 a.m.–4:30 p.m. Sun, closed Mon.

Maps: *USGS Athens West.* Maps also available at the garden's conservatory.

Trail contacts: The State Botanical Garden of Georgia, 2450 South Milledge Ave., Athens 30605; (706) 542-1244; www.uga.edu/botgarden

Finding the trailhead: From Atlanta, travel north on I-85 to GA 316 (exit 106). Follow GA 316 east for 40.0 miles to the intersection with US 78/GA 10 (South Bypass) and turn right (east). At 4.6 miles exit the bypass and turn right (south) on South Milledge Avenue.

Travel for 2.0 miles to the gardens' entrance on the right. **GPS:** N33 54.135' / W83 23.027'

The Hike

From the conservatory plaza, cross the small parking area and descend to the right on paved switchbacks through the Shade Garden. Cross a service road and follow the White Trail as it ascends past annual/perennial and trial garden beds before descending again into woods. The trail climbs to a ridge at 0.6 mile, reaching a fence and deer gate. Cross through the gate, descending to the intersection with the Red Trail. Bear right on the White Trail, and continue to a bridge across a stream. Cross and hike through a bottomland area before climbing to a power line corridor at 0.9 mile.

Reenter the woods on the opposite side, descending to a footbridge. Climb a long switchback to a ridge at 1.2 miles before descending to the outermost point of the White Trail. The path turns sharply left and follows a stream valley, crossing several footbridges, before recrossing the power line corridor at 1.7 miles.

On the opposite side the White Trail descends on switchbacks past a ravine, reaching a creek bridge at 2.1 miles. Cross and climb past two intersections with the Red Trail, reaching the second at 2.4 miles. Continue climbing to the Green Trail, where you reach a shelter with an information board and trail map. Turn right, remaining on the White Trail, and descend a switchback, past the Blue Trail, before turning sharply left above the Middle Oconee River at 2.8 miles.

The White Trail follows the riverbank and floodplain, reaching a bridge over a tributary at 3.4 miles. Ahead, recross the power line corridor (note that the White Trail becomes the Orange Trail at this point) and continue along

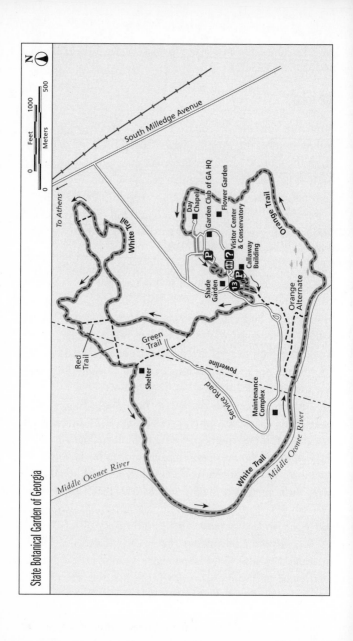

State Botanical Garden of Georgia

the riverbank. After passing an intersection with the Orange Alternate Trail, the path crosses a bridge past a wetland area. The Orange Trail bends sharply left, away from the river, curving along the edge of the wetland before beginning a climb in to wooded hills. Pause to read the informational signs describing the evidence of agricultural use and forest succession along the trail.

Pass a footbridge and access trail, continuing on the Orange Trail. At 4.2 miles cross another bridge, noting evidence of storm-downed trees in the surrounding woods. After a steady ascent, pass back through a deer gate and reenter the main gardens area, reaching the trail terminus at 4.6 miles.

At this point you may cross the parking area and follow steps back to the conservatory plaza. If the nearby Day Chapel is open, walk the short distance to view this beautiful structure nestled in its wooded setting.

Miles and Directions

0.0 Descend from the conservatory plaza to the Shade Garden. (GPS: N33 54.135' / W83 23.027')

0.6 Open the gate to follow the trail.

0.9 Cross and hike through a bottomland area before climbing to a power line corridor.

1.3 Bend left at the outer boundary of the White Trail. (GPS: N33 54.459' / W83 22.790')

2.4 Continue straight, past the Red Trail intersections, to the Green Trail, reconnecting with the White Trail.

2.8 The White Trail bends left at the Middle Oconee River.

3.4 Merge with the Orange Trail at a power line corridor.

3.9 The Orange Trail bends away from the river.

4.6 Reach the trail's terminus at the parking area.

4.9 Return to the conservatory plaza.

14 Stone Mountain Park: Cherokee and Walk-Up Trails

Rising 800 feet above the piedmont hills and encompassing nearly 600 acres of exposed granite, 300-million-year-old Stone Mountain and the surrounding park have long been among Georgia's premier tourist destinations. While the mountain may be best known for the bas-relief carving of Confederate leaders Jefferson Davis, Robert E. Lee, and Stonewall Jackson, the park offers lakes, golf courses, excursion trains, aerial tram, a re-created antebellum plantation, museums, and the Crossroads living history village. The hike described here follows the Cherokee Trail, which encircles the mountain and intersects with the Walk-Up Trail to the summit (a National Historic Trail).

Distance: 7.2-mile lollipop hike

Approximate hiking time: 3–4 hours

Difficulty: More challenging due to distance and terrain

Elevation gain/loss: 358 feet; 824 feet if you hike to the mountain summit

Trail surface: Compacted soil, bare rock

Best season: All year

Canine compatibility: Leashed dogs permitted

Fees and permits: Daily fee or annual pass. Park attractions are individually priced.

Maps: *USGS Stone Mountain and Snellville.* Maps also available from entrance stations and from the park Web site.

Trail contacts: Stone Mountain Park, US 78 E., Stone Mountain 30087; (770) 498-5690 or (800) 401-2407; www.stone mountainpark.com

Finding the trailhead: From I-285, take US 78 (exit 39, Stone Mountain Freeway) and drive east for 12.5 miles to Stone Mountain Park (exit 8), bearing right (south) on the park entrance road. From the entrance station, drive west on Jefferson Davis Drive and bear left (south) on Robert E. Lee Boulevard. At 2.2 miles from the entrance, you will reach the Grist Mill parking area on the left. The hike begins below the parking area by the old mill. **GPS:** N33 48.331' / W84 08.119'

The Hike

From the parking area, follow the access path to the white-blazed Cherokee Trail along Stone Mountain Lake. Cross a terrace by a stone wall before reaching the western side of a nineteenth-century covered bridge at 0.3 mile. Continue straight, crossing two areas of exposed rock.

The path reenters the woods and goes through a rocky area before climbing away from the water to a trail intersection at 1.3 miles. Turn left, across an earthen dam, and bear right along Venable Lake. The trail crosses Stonewall Jackson Drive at 2.2 miles and reenters the woods near a small pond. Descend to a wetland before climbing steps to another dam crossing. On the far side, follow the path to the right of a fenced playground, reaching Robert E. Lee Boulevard at 2.6 miles.

At a trail sign descend stairs to a wooded path. As it approaches the mountain, the trail passes remnants of a long-vanished cabin at 3.0 miles. The path continues past the Nature Gardens Trail before crossing railroad tracks and ascending exposed rock slopes. Follow the white blazes painted on the rock as the trail winds diagonally up the slope to the left (this section may be difficult for small children). After a strenuous climb, cross a service road and

Stone Mountain Park: Cherokee and Walk-Up Trails

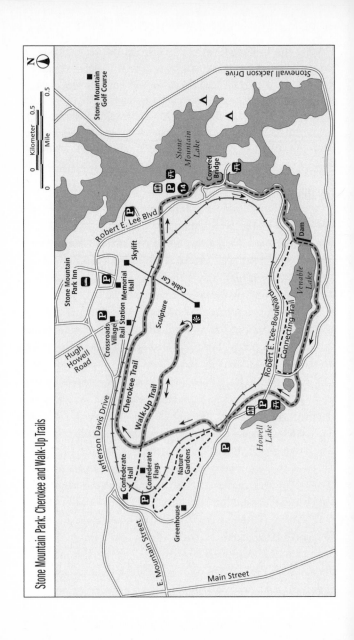

enter a wooded area before reaching the Walk-Up Trail at 3.6 miles.

If you choose to hike to the top of the mountain, turn right and follow the steep path for 0.9 mile to the summit plaza at 4.5 miles. From there, you may enjoy a 360-degree panorama of the park and a spectacular view of the Atlanta skyline. Retrace your steps to the Cherokee Trail and turn right.

The path descends through woods and across open rock, reaching the mountain's base at 5.7 miles. At the intersection of an orange-blazed trail, bear right on the Cherokee Trail as it winds by the railroad tracks and past Crossroads village. From a creek valley, the path climbs to a large meadow (the viewing area for popular evening laser shows) beneath the massive Confederate carving at 6.4 miles.

Cross the meadow, past a reflecting pool, and reenter the woods at a marked trail junction. Turn right on a service road, rejoining the Cherokee Trail ahead on the left. After crossing a bridge and passing a picnic area, the trail bears left and ascends steps to cross the railroad tracks. It then descends, bending right to intersect Robert E. Lee Boulevard at 7.1 miles.

Reenter the woods on the opposite side and bear right, descending along the edge of a picnic area. The trail follows a spillway, carrying water to the gristmill. After reaching the old mill at 7.2 miles, cross the spillway and hike up the paved path to the parking area.

Miles and Directions

0.0 Begin the hike on the white-blazed Cherokee Trail, below the gristmill parking area. (GPS: N33 48.331' / W84 08.119')

0.3 Pass the covered bridge to the rock outcrop.

1.3 Cross Venable Lake dam.

2.2 Cross Stonewall Jackson Drive and reenter the woods by the trail marker. (GPS: N33 47.884' / W84 09.068')

2.6 Cross a dam, and from Robert E. Lee Boulevard reenter the woods at the trail marker. (GPS: N33 48.010' / W84 09.195')

3.1 Beyond the railroad crossing, follow the white blazes up the open rock face of the mountain.

3.6 Turn right at the Walk-Up Trail. (GPS: N33 48.280' / W84 09.359') (**Note:** This trail is uphill—be sure you're in good enough shape to enjoy it.)

4.5 After you reach the mountain summit, retrace your steps back to the Cherokee Trail. (GPS: N33 48.367' / W84 08.760' at summit).

5.7 Bear right at the trail intersection near the mountain's base. (GPS: N33 48.721' / W84 09.302')

6.4 Cross the meadow beneath the carving.

7.1 Cross Lee Boulevard. (GPS: N33 48.484' / W84 08.179')

7.2 Return to the gristmill and your starting point.

15 Davidson-Arabia Mountain Nature Preserve

One of the Atlanta's most unusual trails crosses the exposed granite hills, wetlands, and forests at Arabia Mountain, taking you back nearly a half billion years in time. Arabia Mountain is a monadnock, an outcrop of rock, near Lithonia (Greek for "place of rock"). After nearly a century of quarrying the stone, the Davidson Mineral Company donated the property to DeKalb County for a park in 1973. In 2006 Arabia Mountain, Panola Mountain, and surrounding areas were recognized by the National Park Service as the Arabia Mountain National Heritage Area. Today a PATH Foundation multiuse trail links Arabia and Panola Mountains.

Distance: 5.8-mile hike of interconnected loops

Approximate hiking time: 3 hours

Difficulty: Moderate due to distance and gentle climbs

Elevation gain/loss: 172 feet

Trail Surface: A mix of pavement, compact soil, boardwalks, and exposed rock

Best Season: Spring and fall

Other trail users: PATH trail is open to bicyclists and inline skaters

Canine compatibility: Leashed dogs permitted

Fees and permits: Free

Schedule: Open daily from sunrise to sunset

Maps: USGS Redan and Conyers. Park maps are also available from the nature center, from the Arabia Alliance's Web site, and from DeKalb County's Web site, www.co.dekalb.ga.us/parks/pdf/ArabiaMap.pdf.

Trail contacts: Davidson-Arabian Nature Preserve, 3787 Klondike Rd., Lithonia 30038; (770) 484-3060; www.arabiaalliance.org; sadickie@co.dekalb.ga.us

Finding the trailhead: From Atlanta, follow I-20 east to Evans Mill Road (exit 74). The exit ramp becomes Evans Mill Parkway. At the second traffic light turn right (south) on Evans Mill Road. Soon Evans Mill Road turns right, but continue straight to Woodrow Drive. At 1.1 miles Woodrow ends at Klondike Road. Turn right (south) and follow Klondike Road for 2.2 miles to the park entrance and nature center on the right. There is a satellite parking area further south on Klondike, just past the North Goddard Road intersection. **GPS:** N33 40.344' / W84 06.972'

The Hike

Follow the paved trail behind the nature center to the Arabia Mountain PATH Trail. Turn left and walk for 0.2 mile. Just before reaching a bridge, cross Klondike Road and reenter the woods on an old service road (blocked by large rocks). At 0.6 mile you will turn right at a three-way intersection (continuing straight leads to an old quarry area on the slopes of Arabia Peak) and follow a wooded path to the exposed rock face. There is no clearly blazed trail, so proceed up the moderate slope toward the summit of Bradley Peak, noting the unusual swirl patterns characteristic of ancient Lithonia gneiss.

Reach the 954-foot summit of Bradley Peak (the highest on Arabia Mountain) at 1.0 mile to enjoy a wonderful view. As you descend, follow stacked-stone cairns that mark the path, reaching a parking area at 1.6 miles. Turn right and follow Klondike Road for 0.2 mile to North Goddard Road. Cross with caution and walk a short distance down North Goddard to an emergency-vehicle parking area. Turn right and follow the exposed rock outcrop, ascending gently to the right and staying below an area that was actively quarried for many years.

Turn left on the PATH Trail, crossing a ridge and passing ruins of the quarry office before descending to a boardwalk over a stream area at 2.8 miles. When the boardwalk bends sharply left, descend a stairway to Fern Trail and follow the creek a short distance. At 3.2 miles the trail ascends away from the water and makes a sharp left by Arabia Lake, a pond built to provide water for the quarry.

Beyond the lake the path (now called the Forest Trail) enters a pine and oak forest, crossing shallow ridges on switchbacks before merging with the PATH Trail at 4.0 miles and gently descending. Before reaching the nature center, turn right on a wooded path that follows the route of an old railroad spur line. At a trail fork bear right to reach the exposed rock, noting building ruins on the left as you cross the granite outcrop. Follow stacked stone cairns across the old quarry, reaching Frog Pond at 4.9 miles. A short distance ahead, pass the old quarry office and turn left to rejoin the PATH Trail.

Follow the trail along the route of the old quarry road, past a low stone wall and pillars that once marked the quarry entrance. Soon you will pass the point where you previously crossed Klondike Road toward Bradley Peak. Continue straight, returning to the nature center at 5.8 miles.

Miles and Directions

0.0 Begin the hike behind the nature center parking area, heading toward Arabia Peak. (GPS: N33 40.344' / W84 06.972')

0.2 Cross Klondike Road and enter the woods on an old service road.

0.6 Bear right at the three-way intersection. Reach the exposed rock slope of Bradley Peak.

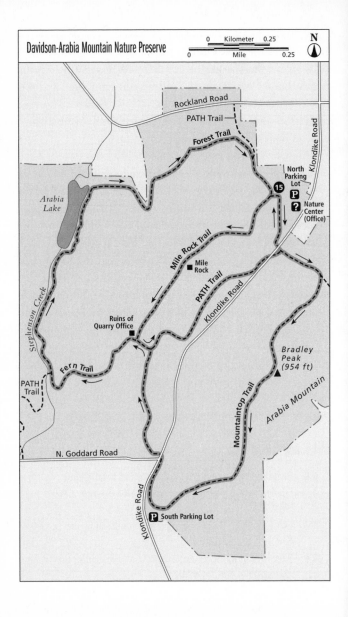

Davidson-Arabia Mountain Nature Preserve

N

Rockland Road

PATH Trail

Forest Trail

Klondike Road

North Parking Lot

15

Nature Center (Office)

Arabia Lake

Mile Rock Trail

Mile Rock

PATH Trail

Klondike Road

Stephenson Creek

Ruins of Quarry Office

Bradley Peak (954 ft)

Fern Trail

Arabia Mountain

PATH Trail

Mountaintop Trail

N. Goddard Road

Klondike Road

South Parking Lot

1.0 Take in the panoramic view atop Bradley Peak. (GPS: N33 39.918' / W84.07.096)

1.6 Turn right on Klondike Road. (GPS: N33 39.596' / W84 07.431')

1.8 Turn right from North Goddard Road to reenter the park.

2.3 Turn left at the intersection with the PATH Trail. (GPS: N33 40.002' / W84 07.437')

2.9 Descend the stairway to the Fern Trail. Follow the stream bed to Arabia Lake. (GPS: N33 40.050' / W84 07.763')

4.0 The Forest Trail merges with the PATH Trail.

4.2 Exit the PATH Trail to the right.

5.0 Rejoin the PATH Trail and turn left.

5.8 Return to the nature center.

16 Panola Mountain State Park

This 1,500-acre park offers visitors an opportunity to explore the exposed rocks and fragile environment of 940-foot-high Panola Mountain. Once called Little Stone Mountain, Panola is a designated National Natural Landmark, as well as a laboratory for geological study. A hike along the 0.75-mile Rock Outcrop and 1.25-mile Micro-watershed Trail offers an excellent introduction to the park and is open during park hours. An optional, guided summit hike is available on a scheduled basis; there is a fee and reservations are recommended. In addition, Panola Mountain Park and nearby Arabia Mountain are linked by a 12-mile section of the Arabia Mountain PATH Trail.

Distance: 2.0 miles in connected loops

Approximate hiking time: 1 hour

Difficulty: Easy to moderate due to distance and terrain

Elevation gain/loss: 110 feet

Trail surface: Compact soil and exposed rock

Best season: All year

Canine compatibility: Leashed dogs permitted on self-guiding trails but prohibited on summit hikes

Fees and permits: Daily parking fee (free on Wed) or annual parks pass

Schedule: Park open daily 7 a.m.–6 p.m. (later in summer). Nature center open daily 8:30 a.m.–5 p.m.

Maps: USGS Redan and Stockbridge. Trail maps available from park Web site and at nature center.

Trail contacts: Panola Mountain State Conservation Park, 2600 GA 155 SW, Stockbridge 30281; (770) 389-7801; www.gastateparks.org

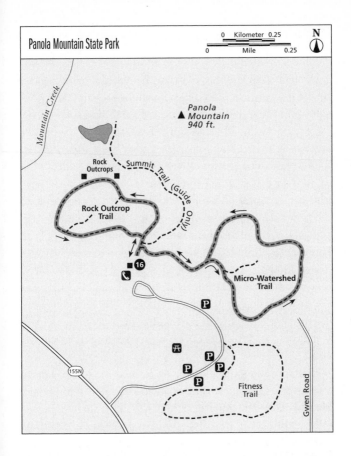

Panola Mountain State Park

0 Kilometer 0.25
0 Mile 0.25

N

Mountain Creek

▲ Panola
Mountain
940 ft.

Rock
Outcrops

Summit Trail (Guide Only)

Rock Outcrop
Trail

16

Micro-Watershed
Trail

P

155N

P

P

P

P

P

Fitness
Trail

Gwen Road

Finding the trailhead: From the intersection of I-75/85 and I-20 in downtown Atlanta, travel 11.1 miles east on I-20 to Wesley Chapel Road (exit 68). Turn right (south) and drive 0.3 mile to the intersection with Snapfinger Road. Turn diagonally left (southeast) and go 1.8 miles to GA 155. Continue straight on GA 155 for 5.0 miles to the park entrance on the left. **GPS:** N33 37.529' / W84 10.298'

The Hike

A hike on the Rock Outcrop (white blaze) and Micro-watershed Trail (red blaze) begins behind the nature center by the information board. Brochures for each trail are available and correspond to signs located along the path.

To follow the Rock Outcrop Trail, continue a short distance to a trail fork and proceed straight so that you follow the loop in a counter-clockwise direction. The path is level to an intersection at 0.3 mile. The trail bends sharply right (the path straight ahead bisects the loop) and descends to the first rock outcrop observation area at 0.4 mile (the trail along here is bordered by wooden rails and stone pillars). Pause here to examine the exposed granite and read the information on Panola Mountain's geology. Gently ascend to a second observation area at 0.5 mile and bear left, past a boardwalk side trail, and descend to a footbridge over an intermittent stream. After ascending on a switchback, you will close the loop and bear right on a return to the starting point.

To continue on the Micro-watershed Trail, turn left on a level path across a service road and through a prescribed burn area. At 0.2 mile bear left and climb steps to a sign with information describing micro-watersheds. Continue to the right and gently descend to the trail loop at 0.3 mile. Descend to the right on stepped-switchbacks to a deep erosion gulley at 0.4 mile. A short side trail to the left leads to a view of the extent of the gulley. Turn right across a bridge, and bend away from the ravine, continuing down on a long switchback. Cross another bridge and reach a lower observation area at 0.6 mile. At this point you may glance upslope to see the extent of the erosion from many years ago.

Proceed a short distance to another observation site and cross the bridge. Begin a steady ascent through hardwood and mixed slope forest areas, reaching the ridge crest at 0.7 mile. You will close the loop at 0.9 mile and retrace your steps to the starting point at 1.2 miles. The two trails combine for a hike of 2.0 miles. A walk along the Fitness Trail will add a mile.

Miles and Directions

0.0 Start at the information board behind the nature center. (GPS: N33 37.529' / W84 10.298')

0.4 Arrive at the first observation area on Rock Outcrop Trail.

0.5 Arrive at the second observation area on Rock Outcrop Trail. (GPS: N33 37.678' / W84 10.445')

0.7 Return to the starting point and Micro-watershed Trail.

1.0 Reach the Micro-watershed Trail loop.

1.1 Cross the bridge over the erosion gulley.

1.3 Arrive at the observation area at the base of the gulley. (GPS: N33 37.382' / W84 10.090')

1.6 Complete the trail loop.

2.0 Arrive back at the starting point.

Option: Guided Hike to Panola Mountain's Summit: The 3.5–5.0-mile, naturalist-guided hike leads through piedmont woodlands, across erosion gullies and ravines, past an old farm pond, and through a river cane restoration area along the South River. From that point, the hike leads up to and across the fragile environment of Panola Mountain's rock face, offering panoramic views of Stone Mountain to the north and Arabia Mountain to the northeast. The route down the mountain is, at times, steep before reentering the woods and descending past large rock outcrops to the farm pond. The path then follows a rolling course back to the nature center. This moderate to strenuous hike takes about 3 hours.

17 Reynolds Nature Preserve

First farmed before the Civil War, this land was purchased in the 1920s by Judge William H. Reynolds, who spent years reclaiming worn-out fields, building ponds, and planting trees. He also added thousands of native azaleas, and for many years visitors traveled great distances to tour the gardens. In 1976 Reynolds donated 130 acres to Clayton County for a public preserve. Federal grant funds were later used to construct a nature center, trails, footbridges, and picnic pavilion. Today the Reynolds Nature Preserve is operated by the Clayton County Parks and Recreation Department.

Distance: 2.8-mile network of intersecting loops
Approximate hiking time: 2 hours
Difficulty: Easy with some hills
Elevation gain/loss: 133 feet
Trail surface: Dirt and wood chips
Best season: All year
Canine compatibility: Leashed dogs permitted
Fees and permits: Free
Land status: Public

Schedule: Grounds open daily from 8 a.m. to dusk. Nature center open 8:30 a.m.–5:30 p.m. Mon–Fri, 9 a.m.–1 p.m. the first Sat of each month.
Maps: *USGS Jonesboro.* Map also available from Web site.
Trail contacts: William H. Reynolds Nature Preserve, 5665 Reynolds Rd., Morrow 30260; (770) 603-4188; http://web.co.clayton.ga.us/reynolds/about.htm

Finding the trailhead: Travel I-75 south to GA 54, Jonesboro Road (exit 233). Turn left and drive north on GA 54 for 0.9 miles to Reynolds Road. Turn left and travel 1.2 miles. The reserve entrance is on the left. **GPS:** N33 36.066' / W84 20.809'

The Hike

From the nature center's Butterfly Garden, follow the Brookside Trail on an easy descent past Dry Pond and on to Big Pond. At 0.4 mile a pier extends from the bank offering a vantage point for observing aquatic life and birds. Continue across the earthen dam and reenter the woods on the Back Mountain Trail. After a short ascent, turn right on the High Springs Trail before descending to an intersection with the Hickory Stump and Crooked Creek Trails at 1.1 miles. Turn right on Crooked Creek, then left on the Burning Heart Trail and ascend. Bear right and descend on a continuation of the Crooked Creek Trail along a fieldstone wall beneath century-old oak trees. You will soon pass through a lush lowland area of rhododendrons and ferns along a stream bed.

Turn left at 1.3 miles and ascend on the Oak Ridge Trail, following the upper slope to the Burning Heart Trail. Turn right and climb steadily to a ridge crest at 1.6 miles. The path begins a gentle descent to the intersection with the Back Mountain Trail, where you will turn right and continue downward. At 1.8 miles you will reach the Crooked Creek Trail intersection. Bear left on the Cypress Springs Trail and cross a stream before ascending. Ahead, a side trail leads out to wetlands along Woodland Pond (0.2 mile round-trip). Continue to a ridge before reaching the Boardwalk Trail at 2.3 miles. Turn right and follow the boardwalk as it bends left along a stream and wetland area. Soon you will exit the woods behind the Reynolds farm house complex, which contains an outdoor classroom, a demonstration garden, and a barn with old farm equipment on display. Turn right and follow the path back to the nature center.

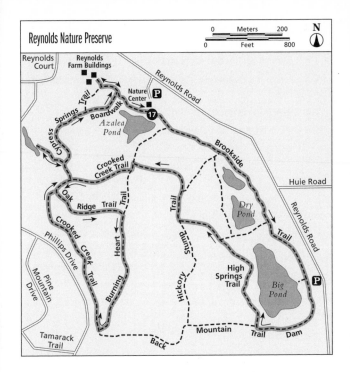

Reynolds Nature Preserve

| 0 | Meters | 200 | **N** |

| 0 | Feet | 800 |

Miles and Directions

0.0 The trail starts behind the nature center. Note the butterfly garden and area designated as a Georgia Native Plants Trail. (GPS: N33 36.066' / W84 20.809')

0.4 Reach the pier extending into the pond. (GPS: N33 35.772' / W84 20.657')

0.5 Ascend into the woods on the Back Mountain Trail.

1.1 Reach the intersection of the Hickory Stump and Crooked Creek Trails. (GPS: N33 35.978' / W84 20.849')

1.3 Turn left on the Oak Ridge Trail.

1.7 Turn right on the Back Mountain Trail. (GPS: N33 35.843' / W84 21.050')

1.8 Turn left on the Cypress Springs Trail.

2.3 Follow the Boardwalk Trail on the loop from Cypress Springs Trail.

2.4 Reach Reynolds' house and complex.

2.8 Arrive back at the nature center.

18 Dauset Trails Nature Center

Created in 1977 by local business and civic leaders Hampton **Dau**ghtry and David **Set**tle, the Dauset Trails Nature Center is a 1,200-acre private nonprofit outdoor education and recreation area adjacent to Indian Springs State Park. The center offers more than 17 miles of hiking and mountain biking trails through a wooded piedmont landscape. Dauset Trails offers nature exhibits, classrooms, picnic pavilions, a group campground, a lakeside chapel, and the Animal Trail, featuring native, non-releasable creatures in fenced habitats. The hiking route described is an excellent introduction to the center's natural beauty.

Distance: 5.8-mile hike of interconnected loops
Approximate hiking time: 3 hours
Difficulty: Moderate due to terrain and distance
Elevation gain/loss: 141 feet
Trail surface: Compacted soil and gravel
Best season: Spring and fall
Other trail users: Mountain bicyclists (Note: Nature center staff urge bicyclists to refrain from riding in wet conditions.)

Canine compatibility: Dogs not permitted
Fees and permits: Free (donations welcome)
Schedule: Nature Center open 9 a.m.–5 p.m. Mon–Sat, noon–5 p.m. Sun. Trails open sunrise to sunset.
Maps: *USGS Indian Springs.* Maps also available at the nature center and on the preserve Web site.
Trail contacts: Dauset Trails Nature Center, 360 Mount Vernon Rd., Jackson 30233; (770) 775-6798; www.dausettrails.com

Finding the trailhead: From Atlanta, follow I-75 south to GA 36 (exit 201). Turn left (east) and drive 3.1 miles to High Falls Road.

Turn right (south) and go 2.4 miles to Mount Vernon Road. Turn left (east), following Mount Vernon for 3.0 miles to the nature center drive on the left. Hikers are urged to park at the gravel entrance 0.1 mile west of the main entrance. The trailhead parking area remains open after the main gates are closed at 5 p.m. **GPS:** N33 13.966' / W83 56.988'

The Hike

(*Note:* Trails are marked by numbered signs at major intersections. Reference maps are available at the center and online.)

From the trailhead parking area, pass the information board and follow the service road a short distance to the intersection of the Bootlegger and Moonshine Trails. Turn right, following the Moonshine Trail as it passes above a ravine, reaching the group camp at 0.5 mile. Continue past the chapel and pavilion to a gravel road and turn right. Cross a bridge and turn right, following the edge of a pond before reentering the woods on the left at 0.7 mile.

Bear right, crossing another bridge, and then right again along the path as it ascends. Continue past another bridge (connection to the Turkey Trot Trail) to signpost 14. Ascend to the Wagon Track Trail at 1.3 miles near the Animal Trails enclosure. Turn left on the Wagon Track Trail and descend through piedmont mixed forest. Follow the hiker symbol at the next intersection and continue to the creek bottom. Turn left, then right, crossing a footbridge by signpost 13. Bend sharply right along a stream before bearing left and ascending to an intersection with a gravel road at 1.7 miles.

Cross the road and reenter the woods on the Wagon Track Trail, descending to a bridge over an intermittent stream, before reaching a creek bottom at 2.1 miles. Turn right on the Pine Mountain Trail (the wrong way sign is for bikers), following the stream a short way before turning from the water near signpost 17 at 2.6 miles. Ascend several ridges to a trail fork and bear left, turning more sharply left by a dry creek bed at 3.0 miles. The trail skirts the edge of a meadow before reaching an intersection with the gravel road at 3.3 miles (signpost 16).

Turn right on the road and descend past the Wagon Track Trail, back to the pond and picnic area. Past the driveway, turn right and cross a meadow, reentering the woods on the Wagon Track Trail (signpost 18). At a four-way intersection, turn right on the Fern Gully Trail, descending on switchbacks to a wetlands area. Continue to a trail intersection by a suspension bridge at 4.4 miles (the path across the bridge leads to the hiking/biking trails in the northern section of the park). Turn left, away from the bridge, following the creek for about 0.1 mile before ascending away from the water. Return to the four-way intersection at 4.7 miles and turn right on the Bootlegger Trail. The path soon passes a meadow before reentering the woods. Bend sharply left, through another meadow, as the path follows the preserve boundary.

You will return to the gravel service road at the end of the Bootlegger Trail at 5.8 miles (signpost 20). The parking area is a short distance to the right.

Miles and Directions

0.0   From the trailhead parking area, follow the service road to the Moonshine Trail. (GPS: N33 13.966' / W83 56.988')

0.5   Pass the group camp, chapel, and pavilion.

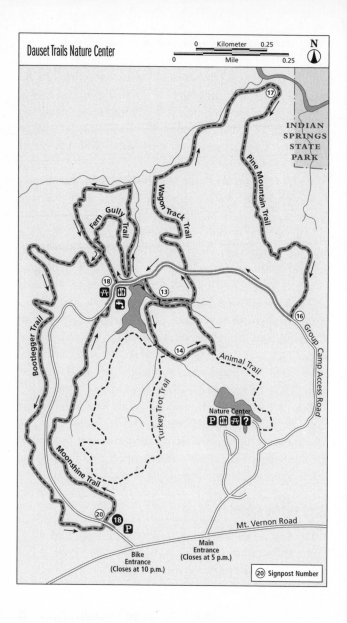

0.7 Cross the pond spillway and follow the path to the right along the pond's edge.

1.3 Turn left on the Wagon Track Trail by the enclosure. (GPS: N33 14.300' / W83 56.748')

1.7 Cross the gravel road and reenter the woods.

2.1 Turn right at the creek bottom.

3.3 Turn right on the gravel road at signpost 16. (GPS: N33 14.372' / W83 56.586')

3.7 Cross the meadow by the picnic area and reenter the woods on the Wagon Track Trail. (GPS: N33 14.462' / W83 56.980')

4.4 Bend left at the suspension bridge.

4.7 At the four-way intersection, turn right on Bootlegger Trail.

5.8 Reach the service road at the end of the Bootlegger Trail. The parking area is on the right.

19 Sweetwater Creek State Park

This park preserves both the natural piedmont landscape and the ruins of the New Manchester Manufacturing Company's mill that operated from 1849 until burned by the Union Cavalry on July 9, 1864. Today the mill's brick walls and mill race serve as reminders of Atlanta's early history and the heartbreak of the Civil War. The park's visitor center features exhibits about the area's natural history and the tragic story of the mill and the people who worked there. In addition, the LEED (Leadership in Energy and Environmental Design)–certified building is among the world's most energy-efficient structures.

Distance: 6.5-mile hike of interconnecting loops
Approximate hiking time: 4 hours
Difficulty: More challenging due to distance
Elevation gain/loss: 389 feet
Trail surface: Compact soil, exposed rock, sandy floodplain
Best season: All year
Canine compatibility: Leashed dogs permitted
Fees and permits: Daily parking fee (free on Wed) or annual pass
Schedule: Daily 7 a.m.–10 p.m.; Visitor Center open 8 a.m.–5 p.m. Thur–Sat
Maps: USGS Austell, Mableton, Ben Hill, and Campbellton. Maps also available at the visitor center and on the park Web site.
Trail contacts: Sweetwater Creek State Conservation Park, 1750 Mount Vernon Rd., Lithia Springs 30122; (770) 732-5871; www.gastateparks.org

Finding the trailhead: Travel west from Atlanta on I-20 for about 12 miles to Thornton Road (exit 44) and turn left (south). In 0.5 mile turn right (west) on Blair's Bridge Road and drive 2.3 miles to Mount Vernon Road. Turn left (south) and go 1.6 miles to the park entrance

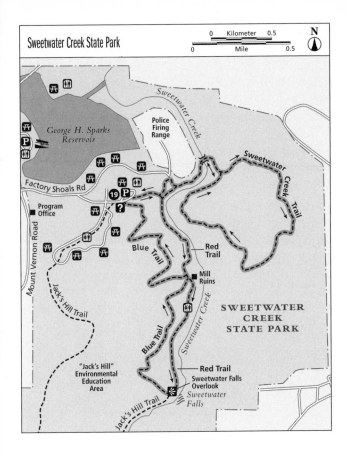

Sweetwater Creek State Park

George H. Sparks Reservoir

Police Firing Range

Sweetwater Creek

Factory Shoals Rd

Program Office

Mount Vernon Road

Jack's Hill Trail

Blue Trail

Red Trail

Mill Ruins

Sweetwater Creek

SWEETWATER CREEK STATE PARK

"Jack's Hill" Environmental Education Area

Blue Trail

Jack's Hill Trail

Red Trail
Sweetwater Falls Overlook
Sweetwater Falls

on Factory Shoals Road. Turn left (east), following the road to the visitor center parking area. **GPS:** N33 45.224' / W84 37.706'

The Hike

Begin your hike from the visitor center parking area by descending on the Red (History) Trail, past the intersection with the Yellow (Sweetwater Creek) Trail, to the creek bank at 0.2 mile. Bear right, following the old mill road to an overlook above a series of shoals. Look below to see remains of the original mill race. Continue another 0.5 mile to an observation platform with an informational sign above the historic mill ruins. Ahead, at the intersection of the Red and Blue Trails, turn left on the Red Trail and descend steps to the creek.

Turn right, following the trail along a very rocky course above the water (be cautious with small children), to a bridge over a stream. Steeply ascend to a bluff with an excellent view of rocky shoals. The path descends along the creek before climbing to a platform overlooking Sweetwater Creek Falls at 1.1 miles. The white-blazed Jack's Hill Trail continues to follow the creek. Follow the Blue (Nature) Trail as it ascends steeply away from the water on wooden steps to the slopes above. The Blue Trail follows the hillside, passing through a lush area of ferns and other undergrowth before rejoining the Red Trail at 1.9 miles. Retrace your steps past the mill and bear left as the Blue Trail forks away from the creek a second time. The path ascends steadily across ridges and stream valleys, reaching the visitor center at 3.2 miles.

To continue the hike, retrace your steps to the Red Trail and descend again to the intersection with the Yellow Trail. Continue straight, descending on the Yellow Trail to a footbridge over a small stream. Turn left across the bridge and follow the path along the floodplain. At 0.7 mile turn right and cross an old automobile bridge (closed) over Sweetwater Creek. On the opposite bank, turn right and descend the steps to the path.

Bear left at the trail fork and ascend, at times steeply, to a ridge at 1.3 miles. From this point, the path traverses several ridges before descending toward the creek along a route marked by large rock outcrops. Reach the creek bottom at 2.1 miles and complete the loop at 2.5 miles. Retrace your steps across the auto bridge, along the floodplain, and over the footbridge.

At the intersection of the Yellow Trail and an unblazed path along the creek, follow the unblazed path a short distance to the Red Trail. Turn right and ascend to the parking area at 3.1 miles. Combining the two loops, the hike at Sweetwater Creek is 6.5 miles.

Miles and Directions

0.0 Begin at the parking area by the visitor center. (GPS: N33 45.224' / W84 37.706)

0.2 Turn right along the old mill road.

0.7 The observation deck above the mill ruins offers a good view of the shoals. At the bottom of the steps, follow the Red Trail.

1.1 The Blue Trail ascends above the falls. (GPS: N33 44.504' / W84 37.509')

1.9 The Blue Trail forks to the left.

3.2 The Blue Trail reaches the visitor center. Retrace your steps on the Red Trail to reach the Yellow Trail.

3.5 Go straight on the Yellow Trail at the intersection.

4.2 Cross the old road bridge over Sweetwater Creek and turn right. (GPS: N33 45.340' / W84 37.346')

4.8 Reach the ridge crest above the creek.

6.0 Complete the Yellow Trail loop.

6.5 Enjoy the outstanding visitor center.

20 McIntosh Reserve

This 527–acre Carroll County park was once the home of
Creek chief William McIntosh. Son of a Scots immigrant
and a Creek princess, McIntosh served under Andrew Jackson in the War of 1812. In 1821 he brought together Creek
and Cherokee leaders to establish a boundary between the
two nations (they met at "Council Bluffs" along the trail by
the Chattahoochee River). Four years later, McIntosh signed
the Treaty of Indian Springs, ceding the final Creek lands in
Georgia to the state. He was later assassinated here by treaty
opponents. His grave is near the site of his farmhouse.

Distance: 6.9-mile circuit of
interconnected loops
Approximate hiking time: 4 hours
Difficulty: More challenging due
to distance and terrain
Elevation gain/loss: 300 feet
Trail surface: Sandy floodplain,
packed dirt, gravel
Best season: Spring and fall
Other trail users: Equestrians
Canine compatibility: Leashed
dogs permitted

Fees and permits: Daily parking fee
Schedule: Open daily 8 a.m.–8
p.m.
Maps: *USGS Whitesburg.* Trail
maps available at the entrance
station.
Trail contacts: McIntosh
Reserve, 1046 West McIntosh
Circle, Whitesburg 30185; (770)
830-5879; www.carrollcountyrec
.com

Finding the trailhead: From Atlanta, travel south on I-85 for
about 37 miles to GA 34 (exit 47). Turn right (north) and drive a
short distance to West Bypass 34 (County 747). Turn right (west)
and drive 4.5 miles to GA 16/North Alternate US 27. Turn right
(north) and go 8.5 miles to Whitesburg. At the traffic circle turn left
(west) and travel 1.5 miles to West McIntosh Circle (watch for a

small road sign). Turn left (south) and drive 1.0 mile to the entrance station. After checking in, go another 0.5 mile to a parking area near the old ranger station. **GPS:** N33 26.537' / W84 57.108'

The Hike

From the old ranger station, cross the road and hike to an observation platform overlooking the Chattahoochee River. Descend through a picnic area and campground to the River Trail, which follows the floodplain. After crossing a footbridge over a stream, you will reach Council Bluffs at 0.6 mile.

At the trail fork bear left on the River Trail, following the edge of a large recreation field. At 1.5 miles the trail bends away from the water and follows the field's edge for another 0.5 mile. After a sharp left around the beaver pond, which is drying out, the path turns right and ascends to the woods. After crossing a ridge descend along a wetlands area before climbing to an intersection at 2.4 miles. Turn right and continue toward the horse-trailer parking area.

Bear left, crossing the edge of the parking lot, and reenter the woods as the path parallels the park road. Cross a ridge at 2.8 miles and descend through a ravine to the far slope, passing the park's maintenance area. Bend right, hiking down to a stream crossing before ascending, a short distance from the park's check-in station, to merge with a gravel service road at 3.3 miles. Continue on the road for about a hundred yards before the trail exits to the left.

Descend on the occasionally rutted path to a creek bottom, bend right, and ascend a moderate slope. The trail follows a series of switchbacks to another gravel road at 3.9 miles. Cross it and descend to a meandering path across several shallow streams surrounded by ferns. At 4.2 miles cross

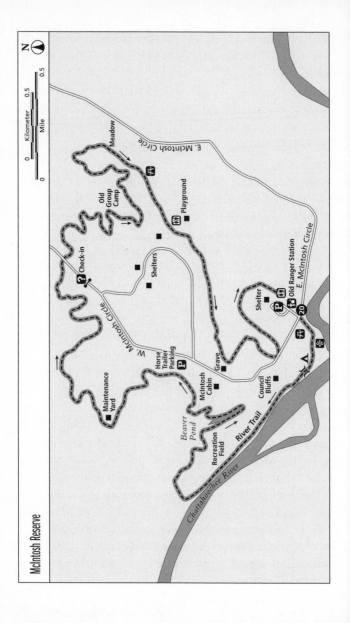

McIntosh Reserve

the park entrance road (West McIntosh Circle) and follow several shallow ridges on a gentle descent to an abandoned group camping area at 4.7 miles.

Turn right, then quickly left, and climb to a ridge. After descending, the trail bends sharply left at the intersection (proceeding straight leads to the entrance station) and meanders through a lowland area. Cross on stones over a stream bed before turning left to cross a bridge over another creek. The path bends sharply right, exiting the woods to a meadow that is often used for recreation. Bear right and hike past a group picnic shelter, small ponds, a playground, and a comfort station.

The trail reenters the woods to the left of a paved road and gently ascends to the right, reaching the edge of a meadow at 6.1 miles. Nearby are Chief McIntosh's grave and the 180-year-old cabin on the site of his home. Across the meadow from the grave site, the trail descends above a deep ravine, reaching a stream crossing on an automobile bridge at 6.5 miles. On the far side, turn left and climb steeply to a ridgetop intersection. Turn right and descend a short distance to your starting point at 6.9 miles.

Miles and Directions

0.0 Begin at the parking area by the old ranger station. (GPS: N33 26.537' / W84 57.108')

0.6 After crossing a footbridge, reach Council Bluffs.

1.5 Bear right at the end of the River Trail. (GPS: N33 26.964' / W84 57.971')

2.4 Bear left at the trail intersection below the horse-trailer parking area. (GPS: N33 26.810' / W84 57.443')

3.3 Merge with the service road. (GPS: N33 27.230' / W84 57.222')

4.2 Cross the park entrance road. (GPS: N33 27.386' / W84 56.952')

5.6 At the edge of a field, bear right toward the group shelter. (GPS: N33 26.952' / W84 56.994')

6.1 Pause at Chief McIntosh's grave and home site. (GPS: N33 26.743' / W84 57.365')

6.9 Arrive back at the parking area.

Hiking Groups

Interested in discovering favorite hiking destinations with other like-minded adventurers? Consider joining one of the following groups.

Atlanta Outdoor Club: Outdoors-oriented social organization for active adults of all ages. There are no membership dues and events are fee-based and require a reservation. (www.atlantaoutdoorclub.com)

Georgia Walkers: A membership organization affiliated with the American Volkssport Association (www.ava.org). (http://georgiawalkers.homestead.com)

Hotlanta Adventures: This group targets active adults ages eighteen to forty. There is a fee for activities. (www.hotlanta adventures.org)

Mosaic Outdoor Club of Georgia: Associated with Mosaic Outdoor Clubs of America, this group sponsors activities for Jewish adults and families. (http://mosaicga.com)

Walking Club of Georgia: Sanctioned by U.S. Track and Field, this club hosts walks and hikes and also supports race-walking competitions. (www.walkingclubofgeorgia.com)

Wilderness Network of Georgia: This membership organization offers outdoor activities for members of the area's gay community. (www.wildnetga.org)

Women's Outdoor Network (WON): This membership organization offers group outdoor recreational opportunities for women eighteen or older. (www.wonatlanta.com)

About the Authors

Ren Davis is a native Atlantan with a lifelong interest in the city's and region's history. He is also an avid hiker and backpacker whose adventures include section-hiking the Appalachian Trail with friends. In addition to work as an executive for Emory Healthcare, he has been a freelance writer and photographer for more than twenty years. He has authored numerous travel articles for newspapers and magazines.

Helen Davis is a native of Lewistown, Pennsylvania, and has called Atlanta home since 1974. She is an elementary school educator, with training in special needs education, and she has taught both in Atlanta public schools and private schools. She especially enjoys helping students explore Atlanta.

The couple has authored several guidebooks including *Atlanta Walks* and *Georgia Walks,* and most recently *Best Hikes Near Atlanta* for FalconGuides.

WHAT'S SO SPECIAL ABOUT UNSPOILED, NATURAL PLACES?

Beauty Solitude Wildness Freedom Quiet Adventure
Serenity Inspiration Wonder Excitement
Relaxation Challenge

There's a lot to love about our treasured public lands, and the reasons are different for each of us. Whatever your reasons are, the national **Leave No Trace** education program will help you discover special outdoor places, enjoy them, and preserve them—today and for those who follow. By practicing and passing along these simple principles, you can help protect the special places you love from being loved to death.

THE PRINCIPLES OF **LEAVE NO TRACE**

- Plan ahead and prepare
- Travel and camp on durable surfaces
- Dispose of waste properly
- Leave what you find
- Minimize campfire impacts
- Respect wildlife
- Be considerate of other visitors

Leave No Trace is a national nonprofit organization dedicated to teaching responsible outdoor recreation skills and ethics to everyone who enjoys spending time outdoors.

To learn more or to become a member, please visit us at www.LNT.org or call (800) 332-4100.

Leave No Trace, P.O. Box 997, Boulder, CO 80306